The Autobiography

of a

Sexually Emancipated Communist Woman

THE AUTOBIOGRAPHY
OF A
SEXUALLY EMANCIPATED
COMMUNIST WOMAN

ALEXANDRA KOLLONTAI

EDITED WITH AN AFTERWORD
BY IRING FETSCHER

TRANSLATED BY SALVATOR ATTANASIO

HERDER AND HERDER

1971
HERDER AND HERDER   NEW YORK
232 Madison Avenue, New York 10016

Original edition: *Autobiographie*
einer sexuell emanzipierten Kommunistin,
Munich, Verlag Rogner & Bernhard, 1970

Library of Congress Catalog Card Number: 77-165502

Contents

FOREWORD
BY GERMAINE GREER

In this the era of the New Left in the Western world, when
political theorists are seeking in the earliest formulations and
ideological battles of Marxism the basic premisses of their own
revolutionary analysis of the capitalist societies in which they
live, we particularly need to discover the despised and rejected
political credo of Alexandra Kollontai. Kollontai herself was
eventually persuaded that her ideas had little historical relevance
to the state of the Russian nation, and uncomplainingly accepted
distinguished obscurity as a member of the Russian legation in
Oslo and eventually ambassadress. However discreet she may
have become, her basic convictions never changed, for she never
renounced them either. She served the Russian people patiently
and unsparingly throughout her life, out of a deep and selfless
loyalty to a regime which rejected her ideas and accepted her
service. It is difficult to explain the urge to write an autobiography in the first place, without assuming some tenacious
desire to justify herself and her views; but when her ego comes into
conflict with Party policy or dogma, she rigorously stifles it. In this
edition, which includes all Kollontai's elisions and emendations,
one can follow this drama page by page. More cynical readers
may decide that fear of liquidation drives Kollontai's blue pencil,
but I prefer to think that her self-censorship springs in part from
a loftier impulse, the genuine belief that what is achieved by *us*
is much more interesting and worthwhile than what is achieved
by *me*. Kollontai is tacitly recognizing the fact that without the
revolutionary masses who created the extraordinary situation in
Russia in 1917 her accomplishments would have been negligible;
her implied critique of individualism is not merely prompted
by fear but by fervent belief in "magnificent illusions (deleted),

plans, ardent initiatives to improve life, to organize the world anew, . . . the real romanticism of the Revolution."

But behind the deletions and self-censorship we can discern the outlines of this woman's bitter struggle to promote the sexual revolution, without which she saw clearly that petty bourgeois moral standards would again prevail and the authoritarian family continue to underprop the authoritarian and bureaucratic state. Her efforts to democratize the Party, by pressing for the recognition of workers' control and direct participation in policy making and decisions in industry, are part of the same consistent radical outlook. However popular her sexual theories were when she explained them to her audiences, they were within the Party the subjects of heated debate and eventually ridicule. Her concern that the dictatorship of the proletariat should be a practical reality resulted in her being branded a syndicalist, a jibe which she passionately refuted by reference to the words of Marx and Lenin themselves. While pragmatic politicians strengthened the authority of the Bolshevik government, she clung to anti-authoritarian sentiments:

There can be no self-activity without freedom of thought and opinion, for self-activity manifests itself not only in initiative, action and work, but in independent thought as well. We give no freedom to class activity, we are afraid of criticism, we have ceased to rely on the masses, hence we have bureaucracy with us. That is why the Workers' Opposition considers that bureaucracy is our enemy, our scourge, and the greatest danger to the future of the Communist Party itself.[1]

Kollontai's prophetic words on behalf of the Workers' Opposition are relatively well-known, for her pamphlet has been translated and published three times at least in the English-speaking

1. *The Workers' Opposition*, Reading, E. Morse, 1962, p. 35.

world; in America by the Wobblies in the year that it was written, in England by Dreadnought Publishers in 1923, and again by E. Morse of Reading as Solidarity Pamphlet No. 7 in 1962. But Kollontai's feminism is much less familiar. The Library of Congress and the British Museum both hold *Society and Maternity* in Russian, but the *Social Foundations of the Women's Question* is as good as unavailable. *The New Morality and the Working Class* appeared as *La Femme Nouvelle et la Classe Ouvriere,* one of the Cahiers de l'Eglantine, in 1932.

In her autobiography Kollontai is reticent about her theories of morality and sexuality and even her references to women's liberation are guarded and unemphatic. On the first page, she states as an aim of her life, the "setting in bold relief that which concerns the women's liberation struggle and further the social significance which it has," but this is deleted to emphasizing "that which has an importance for the solution of the social problems of our time, and which also includes the problem of complete women's liberation." The inertness of her phraseology may not be entirely attributed to the vicissitudes of translation, for one is struck throughout her biography with the turgidity of her style compared to the rhapsodic writing of *The New Woman,* written in more optimistic times. The most massive elisions in her brief text relate to the double standard of morality and conventional marriage, to love and to criticism of the Party's attitude to such things. She was moved to write of her impressions in 1905, "I realized for the first time how little our Party concerned itself with the fate of the women of the working class and how meagre was its interest in women's liberation," but her ruthless blue pencil strikes it through.

Again, truth bade her write, "For our Soviet marriage law,

separated from the church to be sure, is not essentially more progressive than the same laws which after all exist in other progressive democratic countries," and loyalty prompted her to erase it. The extreme opprobrium which already attached in 1926 to theories of sexual and ethical revolution did not diminish as the years passed. Wilhelm Reich was excluded from the German Communist Party in 1932 and the Institute for Marxism/Leninism in Berlin has omitted all mention of the Sexpol movement from its massive historical study of the German workers' movement. Some insight into the pressures behind this obliteration may be got from Reich's *The Sexual Revolution,* which implies what Kollontai would not let herself believe, that repression of the movement towards a new sexual morality is the first symptom of betrayal of the revolution. While it is true that "women's liberation could take place only as a result of the victory of a new social order and a different economic system," as Kollontai early understood, it is also true that without realigning sexual and family relationships in a new, collective and cooperative way, the new socio-economic system will soon come to resemble the old. As Kollontai correctly foretold in *The Workers' Opposition,* State Capitalism and Monopoly Capitalism have come to resemble each other in all significant respects from the workers' point of view.[2] In her autobiography Kollontai also crosses out references to her early misgivings about the way in which the Bolshevik pressure group related to the great mass of workers. By way of explaining her late entry into the ranks, she wrote humbly, "It seemed to me as if they did not attach sufficient importance to the development of the working-class movement in 'breadth and

2. *Ibid.,* p. 3.

depth'," but even such a guarded statement cannot be allowed to stand.

More distressing perhaps to the women's liberationist in search of conscious-raising is her strange reluctance to expatiate upon love and her own old-fashioned femininity. When she speaks of her abiding romantic desire for a man's love and comradeship turning into disappointment, "since the friend saw in me only the feminine element which he tried to mould into a willing sounding board for his own ego," she gives voice to the dilemma and the confrontation out of which the new left-wing women's movement has been born. Reading her curt words about shaking off "the chains of community," we search in vain for some clue to the way in which she stiffened up her will to counter-act the effect of her own and centuries of conditioning, how much pain resulted, how she bore it and what the consolations might have been, how she coped with the contradictions of her own parent-hood. Abashed even by having revealed so very little, Kollontai noted it for deletion. Perhaps she thought that such struggles had already been abolished by the admission of women to labor and the professions in Russia. "We, the older generation, did not yet understand, as most men do and as young women are learning today, that work and the longing for love can be harmoniously combined, so that work remains as the main goal of existence." In these days of the declining prestige of the female professions in Russia, and the development of various patterns of discrimination against women in the work force, we know that this assumption is too sanguine by a great deal. Reading the chapter of *The New Morality and the Working Class* included in this edition, one is struck by the contemporary relevance of the new woman's priorities, "to protest against the universal servitude of women in the State, the family, society." "She seeks neither the substance nor the goal of life in love, but only that which most men seek for in it: 'diversion, poetry, light.' But she herself does not recognize any power over herself, over her 'ego' on the part of the beloved man."

Kollontai herself voices doubts about the attractiveness of this new way of life to women brought up in the inauthentic but persuasive image of the bewitching women of the past, but behind the chaste paean to work throbs a certitude of a love more exciting, more consuming than any romantic obsession with a single love object. She calls it "harmony," "the polytonal symphony of life"; she refers gingerly to the peculiar sexual mores of women like migrant workers, who have always taken love where they found it, her prose bristling with awareness of the prejudice against female promiscuity. The revolutionary ideal of a fusion of the oceanic with the erotic impulse finds fitful expression: "If one must forget oneself, then I would rather do it not just for one person alone, by preparing a good noon meal and a restful slumber for him; if such be the case, I will grant all that also to such-and-such other unhappy ones." She refers to her own problem of misdirected energies, the problem of the "old breed" who are still numerous on this earth, "the atavistic inclination to be the 'shadow of the husband', his echo . . . As though she had no worth of her own, as though her personality was to be appraised only according to the relations of men to her." "How difficult she will find it to convince herself that a woman must reckon self-renunciation as a sin, even a renunciation for the sake of the beloved, and for the sake of the power of love." She speaks feelingly too of those obsessive passions which do not enrich the soul, but impoverish it and dry it out.

The greatest drama of Kollontai's life was not any of her love relationships, but the tragedy of her relations with the Party. She compresses it into two tiny, pain-filled sentences: "Now began a dark time of my life . . . There were differences of opinion in the Party." Behind the bald words lies the story of her resignation from the post of People's Commissar and the gradual abandonment of projects for replacing the old patriarchal family, of the children's homes for all children and not just orphans and the nationalization of motherhood. "Our party, matured and tempered in the struggle of the revolution, was permitted to be carried away from the direct road in order to journey along the roundabout path of adaptation, formerly condemned and severely branded as 'opportunism.'" In the same year that *The New Morality and the Working Class* and *The Workers' Opposition* appeared, Trotsky's troops shot down the workers of Kronstadt. The cause of left-radical opposition within the beloved Partry had been defeated. In the Spring of 1922 the Eleventh Party Congress, besides appointing Joseph Stalin General Secretary of the Party, ordered a special commission "to investigate the activities of the Workers' Opposition." Kollontai's lover, Alexander Shylapnikov, was to fall victim to a purge. In October 1922, Kollontai was sent to work for the Russian legation in Oslo, an appointment that must have meant nothing but prestigious banishment and defeat to her. She was probably fortunate in not meeting with a harsher punishment. Perhaps she was accorded special consideration as a woman (a thought which she would have found deeply repugnant), considered to have been unduly swayed by Shylapnikov. Perhaps her comrades remembered her old friendship with Lenin and recognized that her criticisms of present policy were in good faith, however flighty or unrealistic or irrelevant they might also have condescended to think them. That she considered her life as a revolutionary was over we can judge from the fact that she wrote her autobiography in 1926, full twenty-six years before she died. In it she promised that she would one day write the story of her struggles during the years 1918–22, when the events were less fresh and painful in her memory, but as far as we can ascertain she never did.

Now that an international revolutionary women's movement is developing on a scale that would have delighted Kollontai with her democratic concern for breadth and depth, we may break through the veil of her modesty and selflessness in order to write a chapter in our own history, or "herstory" as some women's groups prefer to call it. It is to be hoped that this publication of her autobiography will be the spur to the undertaking of the much greater task of reassembling her writings, so much of them popular and ephemeral, so that her chosen life's work can be rescued from obscurity and contempt.

Prefatory Note

This is the first time that the complete autobiography which Alexandra Kollontai wrote in 1926 has been published. The sentences and paragraphs in italics were crossed out in the galley-proofs and left out in her time. Variants were indicated in footnotes which likewise were rejected and crossed out. The reader thus will have an idea of the extent and the intensity of corrections made by the author under the pressure of the gradually sharpening Stalinist control.

"The New Woman" is a chapter from Mme. Kollontai's book *The New Morality and the Working Class (Die neue Moral und die Arbeiterklasse)* published in Berlin in 1920.

THE AUTOBIOGRAPHY
OF A SEXUALLY
EMANCIPATED COMMUNIST WOMAN

The Aims and Worth of My Life

Nothing is more difficult than writing an autobiography. What should be emphasized? Just what is of general interest? It is advisable, above all, to write honestly and dispense with any of the conventional introductory protestations of modesty. For if one is called upon to tell about one's life so as to make the events that made it what it became useful to the general public, it can mean only that one must have already wrought something positive in life, *accomplished a task that people recognize*.[1] Accordingly it is a matter of forgetting that one is writing about oneself, of making an effort to abjure one's ego so as to give an account, as objectively as possible, of one's life in the making and of one's accomplishments. I intend to make this effort but whether it will turn out successfully is something else again. At the same time I must confess that, in a certain sense, this autobiography poses a problem for me. For by looking back while prying, simultaneously, into the future, I will also be presenting to myself the most crucial turning points of my being and accomplishments. *In this way I* [2a] *may succeed in setting into bold relief that which concerns the women's liberation struggle and, further, the social significance which it has*.[2]

1. Author's correction: created something which is recognized by society.
2a. perhaps
2. Author's correction: to emphasize that which has an importance for the solution of the social problems of our time, and which also includes the great problem of complete women's liberation. Author's note with respect to 2: delete

That I ought not to shape my life according to the given model, that I would have to grow beyond myself in order to be able to discern my life's true line of vision was an awareness that was mine already in my youngest years. *At the same time I was also aware*[3] that in this way I could help my sisters to shape their lives, in accordance not with the given traditions but with their own free choice to the extent, of course, that social and economic circumstances permit. I always believed that the time inevitably must come when woman will be judged by the same moral standards applied to man. *For it is not her specific feminine virtue that gives her a place of honor in human society, but the worth of the useful mission accomplished by her,*[4a] *the worth of her personality as human being,* as citizen,[4b] *as thinker, as fighter. Subconsciously this motive was the leading force of my whole life and activity. To go my way, to work, to struggle, to create side by side with men,* and to strive for the attainment of a universal human goal[4c] (for nearly thirty years, indeed, I have belonged to the[4d] Communists) *but, at the same time, to shape my personal, intimate life as a woman according to my own will* and according to the given laws of my nature.[4e] *It was this that conditioned my* line of vision.[4f] *And*[4g] *in fact I have*[4h] *succeeded in structuring my intimate life according to my own standards and*

3. Author's correction: I had a certain presentiment
4a. for society
4b. as creative worker
4c. who fought for the realization of our social ideals
4d. Socialists—now communists
4e. crossed out
4f. world-view
4g. I believe
4h. always

I make no secret of my love experiences[4i] *anymore than does a* man.[4k] *Above all, however, I never let my feelings, the joy or pain of love take the first place in my life inasmuch as creativity, activity, struggle always occupied the foreground.* I managed to become a member of a government cabinet, of the first Bolshevik cabinet in the years 1917/18. I am also the first woman ever to have been appointed ambassadress, a post which I occupied for three years and from which I resigned of my own free will.[41] *This may serve to prove that woman certainly can stand above the conventional conditions of the age. The World War, the stormy, revolutionary spirit now prevalent in the world in all areas has greatly contributed to blunting the edge of the unhealthy, overheated double standard of morality. We are already accustomed not to make overly taxing demands, for example,[4m] on actresses and women belonging to the free professions in matters relating to their married life. Diplomacy, however, is a caste which more than any other maintains its old customs, usages, traditions, and, above all, its strict ceremonial. The fact that a woman, a "free," a single woman was recognized in this position without opposition shows that the time has come when all human beings will be equally appraised according to their activity and their general human dignity. When I was appointed as Russian envoy to Oslo, I realized that I had thereby achieved a victory* not only for

4i. when once love came, I have my relations to the man

4k. as men do

4l. As was shown later, my private life, which I did not shape according to the traditional model, was no hindrance when in all seriousness it was a question of utilizing my energies for a new State [the Soviet Republic] and of functioning first as a member of the first Soviet cabinet, later as ambassadress.

4m. for example (crossed out)

myself, but[4n] *for women* in general[4o] *and indeed, a victory over their worst enemy,* that is to say,[4p] over *conventional morality and conservative concepts of marriage. When on occasion I am told that it is truly remarkable[4r] that a woman has been appointed to such a responsible position,* I always[4s] *think to myself that in the final analysis, the principal victory as regards women's liberation does not lie in this fact alone.* Rather, *what is of a wholly special significance here is that a woman,* like myself,[4t] who *has settled scores with the double standard and* who has never concealed it,[4u] *was accepted into a caste which to this very day staunchly upholds tradition and pseudo-morality. Thus the example of my life can also serve* to dispel[4v] the[4w] *old goblin of the double standard also from the lives of other women.* And this *is a most crucial point of my own existence, which has a certain social-psychological worth and* contributes to the liberation struggle of working women.[4] To avoid any misunderstanding,

4n. crossed out
4o. crossed out
4p. : the
4r. "truly remarkable" (in quotes)
4s. privately
4t. crossed out
4u. crossed out
4v. can be dispelled (and crossed out)
4w. that
    Author's note with respect to 4: delete completely
    Author's new note: Instead of deleting
    For it is not her specific womanish virtue that gives her a place of honor in human society, but the worth of her useful work accomplished for society, the worth of her personality as human being, as creative worker, as citizen, thinker, or fighter. To go my way, to create, to fight side by side with men for the realization of our social ideals (indeed for almost thirty years I belonged to the communists), but, at the same time, to shape my personal life as a woman according to my will.
    Subconsciously this was the guiding force of my whole life and activity .

however, it should be said here that I am still far from being the type of the positively new women who take their experience as females with a relative lightness and, one could say, with an enviable superficiality, whose feelings and mental energies are directed upon all *other things*[5] in life *but sentimental love feelings.*[6] After all I still belong to the generation of women who grew up at a turning point in history. Love with its many disappointments, with its tragedies and eternal demands for perfect *happiness*[7] still played a very great role in my life. An all-too-great role! It was an expenditure of precious time and energy, fruitless and, in the final analysis, utterly worthless. We, the women of the past generation, did not yet[8] understand how to be free. The whole thing was an absolutely incredible squandering of our mental energy, a diminution of our labor power which was dissipated in barren emotional experiences. It is certainly true that we, myself as well as many other activists, militants and working women contemporaries, were able to understand that love was not the main goal of our life and that we knew how to place work at its center. Nevertheless we would have been able to create and achieve much more had our energies not been fragmentized in the eternal struggle with *our egos and with*[9] our feelings for another. It was, in fact, an eternal defensive war against the intervention of the male into our ego, a struggle revolving around the problem-complex: work or marriage and love?

Above all, however, I never let my feelings, joy in love, or sorrow take the first place in my life: productive work, activity, struggle always stood in the foreground.

5. Author's correction: primarily upon all other areas
6. Author's correction: and are not guided by sentimental love-feelings
7. Author's correction: "spiritual community"
8. Author's correction: inwardly, in the mind
9. crossed out

7

We, the older generation, did not yet understand, as most men do and as young women are learning today, that work and the longing for love can be harmoniously combined *so that work remains as the main goal of existence.*[10] Our mistake was that *each time we succumbed to the belief that we had finally found the one and only in the man we loved,* the person with whom we believed we could blend our soul, one who was ready fully to recognize us as a spiritual-physical force.[11]

But *over and over again things turned out differently, since*[12] the man always tried to impose his ego upon us and adapt us fully to his purposes. Thus despite everything the inevitable inner rebellion ensued, over and over again since love became a fetter. We felt enslaved and tried to loosen the love-bond. And after the eternally recurring struggle with the beloved man, we finally tore ourselves away and rushed toward freedom. Thereupon we were *again*[13] alone, *unhappy,*[14] lonesome, but free— free to pursue our beloved, chosen ideal . . . work.

Fortunately young people, the present generation, no longer have to go through this kind of struggle which is absolutely unnecessary to human society. Their abilities, their work-energy will be reserved for their creative activity. *Thus the existence of barriers will become a spur.*[15]

It is essential that I relate some details here about my private life. My childhood was a very happy one, judging by outward

10. so that only a very subordinate place remains available to love
11. Author's correction: unreservedly gave our entire ego to the beloved man in the hope that thereby we could attain a complete spiritual harmony.
12. crossed out
13. crossed out
14. crossed out
15. crossed out

circumstances. My parents belonged to the *old* Russian *nobility*.[16]
I was the only child born of my mother's second marriage
(mother was separated and I was born outside the second marriage, and then adopted). I was the youngest, the most spoiled,
and the most coddled member of the family. This, perhaps, was
the root cause of the protest against everything around me that
very early burgeoned within me. Too much was done for me in
order to make me happy: I had no freedom of maneuver either
in the children's games I played or in the desires that I wanted
to express. At the same time *I wanted to be free.*[17] I wanted to
express desires on my own, to shape my own little life. My
parents were well-to-do. There was no luxury in the house, but
I did not know the meaning of privation. Yet I saw how other
children were forced to give up things, and I was particularly
and painfully shocked by the little peasant children who were
my playmates (we lived almost always in the countryside, on the
estate of my grandfather, who was a Finn). Already as a *small*[18]
child I criticized[19] the injustice of adults and *I experienced as a
blatant* contradiction[20] the fact that everything was offered to me
whereas so much was denied to the other children. *My criticism
sharpened as the years went by and the feeling of revolt against
the many proofs of love around me grew apace.*[21] Already early
in life I had eyes for the social injustices prevailing in Russia. I
was never sent to school because my parents lived in a constant
state of anxiety over my health and they could not endure the

16. Author's correction: old Russian landowner (class)
17. crossed out
18. Author's correction: experienced
19. crossed out
20. Author's correction: painfully felt the
21. crossed out

thought that I, like all other children, should spend two hours daily far from home. My mother probably also had a certain horror of the liberal influences with which I might come into contact at the high school. Mother, of course, considered that I was already sufficiently critically[22] inclined. Thus I received my education at home under the direction of a proficient, clever tutoress who was connected with Russian revolutionary circles. I owe very much to her, Mme. Marie Strakhova. I took[23] the examinations qualifying me for admission to the university when I was barely sixteen (*in 1888*)[24] and thereafter I was expected to lead the life of a "young society woman."[25] Although my education had been unusual and caused me much harm (for years I was extremely shy and utterly inept in the practical matters of life), it must nevertheless be said that my parents were by no means reactionaries. On the contrary, they were even[26] rather progressive for their time. But they held fast to traditions where it concerned the child, the young person under their roof. My first bitter struggle against these traditions revolved around the idea of marriage. I was supposed to make a *good match*[27] and mother was bent upon marrying me off at a very early age. My oldest sister, at the age of nineteen, had contracted marriage with a highly placed gentleman who was nearly *seventy*.[28] I revolted against this *marriage of convenience,* this marriage for money[29]

22. Author's correction: "rebelliously"
23. Author's correction: in St. Petersburg
24. crossed out
25. crossed out
26. Author's correction: liberal
27. Author's correction: "good match" (in quotes)
28. Author's correction: sixty
29. Author's correction: "marriage of convenience" and "marriage for money" (in quotes)

and wanted to marry only for love, *out of a great passion*.[30] Still very young, and against my parents' wishes, I chose my cousin, an impecunious young engineer whose name, Kollontai, I still bear today. My maiden name was Domontovich. The happiness of my marriage lasted hardly three years. I gave birth to a son. Although I personally raised my child with *great care*,[31] motherhood was never the kernel of my existence. A child had not been able to draw the bonds of my marriage tighter. I still loved my husband, but the happy life of a housewife and spouse became for me a "cage." More and more my *sympathies, my*[32] interests turned to the revolutionary working class of Russia. I read voraciously. I zealously studied *all*[33] social questions, attended lectures, and worked in semi-legal societies for the enlightenment of the people. These were the years of the flowering of Marxism in Russia (1893/96). Lenin at that time was only a novice in the literary and revolutionary arena. George Plechanov was the leading mind of the time. I stood close to the materialist conception of history, since in early womanhood I had inclined towards the realistic school. I was an enthusiastic follower of Darwin and Boelsches. A visit to the big and famous Krengolm textile factory, which employed 12,000 workers of both sexes, decided my fate. I could not lead a happy, peaceful life when the working population was so terribly enslaved. I simply had to join this movement. At that time this led to differences with my husband, who felt that my inclinations constituted an act of personal defiance directed against him. I left husband and child

30. "great passion" (in quotes)
31. crossed out
32. crossed out
33. Author's correction: the

and journeyed to Zurich in order to study political economy under Professor Heinrich Herkner. Therewith[34] began my conscious life on behalf of the revolutionary goals of the working-class movement. When I came back to St. Petersburg—now Leningrad—in 1899, I joined the illegal Russian Social Democratic Party. I worked as a writer and propagandist. The fate of Finland, whose independence and relative freedom were being threatened by the reactionary policy of the Czarist regime at the end of the '90's, exercised a wholly special power of attraction upon me. Perhaps my particular gravitation towards Finland resulted from the impressions I received on my grandfather's estate during my childhood. I actively espoused the cause of Finland's national liberation. Thus my first *extensive*[35] scientific work in political economy was a *comprehensive investigation*[36] of the living and working conditions of the Finnish proletariat *in relation to industry*.[37] The book appeared in 1903 in St. Petersburg. My parents had just died, my husband and I had been living separately for a long time, and only my son remained in my care. Now I had the opportunity to devote myself completely to my *aims:*[38] to the Russian revolutionary movement and to the working-class movement *of the whole world.*[39] Love, marriage, family, all were secondary, transient matters. They were there, they intertwine with my life over and over again. But as great as was my love for my husband, immediately it transgressed a cer-

34. Author's correction: at that time; second correction: then
35. Author's correction: more comprehensive [in German *grosse, grossere—tr.*]
36. Author's correction: studies on the
37. crossed out
38. Author's correction: to my work
39. crossed out

12

tain limit in relation to my feminine proneness to make sacrifice, rebellion flared in me anew. I had to go away, I had to break with the man of my choice, otherwise (this was a subconscious feeling in me) I would have exposed myself to the danger of losing my selfhood. It must also be said that not a single one of the men who were close to me has ever had a direction-giving influence on my inclinations, strivings, or my world-view. On the contrary, most of the time I was the guiding spirit. I acquired my view of life, my political line from life itself, and in uninterrupted study *from*[40] books.

In 1905, at the time the so-called first revolution in Russia broke out, after the famous Bloody Sunday, I had already acquired a reputation in the field of economic and social literature. And in those stirring times, when all energies were utilized in the storm of revolt, it turned out that I had become very popular as an orator. Yet in that period *I realized for the first time how little our Party concerned itself with the fate of the women of the working class and how meager was its interest in women's liberation. To be sure a very strong bourgeois women's movement was already in existence in Russia. But my Marxist outlook pointed out to me with an illuminating clarity that* women's liberation[41] could take place only as the result of the victory of a new social order and a different economic system. Therefore I threw myself into the struggle *between the Russian*[42] suffragettes and strove with all my might to induce the working-class move-

40. Author's correction: and
41. Author's correction: I realized that in Russia little had yet been done to draw women workers into the liberation struggle. To be sure a quite strong bourgeois women's movement already existed in Russia at that time. But, as a Marxist, it was clear to me that the lib-
42. Author's correction: against the bourgeois-minded

13

ment to include the woman question as one of the aims of its struggle *in its program*.[43] It was *very difficult*[44] to win my fellow *members*[45] over to this idea. I was completely isolated with my ideas and demands. Nevertheless in the years 1906–1908 I won a small group of women Party comrades over to my plans. I[46] wrote[47] an article published in the illegal press in 1906 in which *for the first time*[48] I set forth the demand to call the working-class movement into being in Russia through systematic Party work. In Autumn of 1907 we opened up the first Working Women's Club. Many of the members of this club, who were still very young workers at that time, now occupy important posts in the new Russia and in the Russian Communist Party (K. Nicolaieva, Marie Burke, etc.). One result of my *activity in connection with the women workers,*[49] but especially of my political writings—among which was a pamphlet on Finland containing the call to rise up against *the Czarist Duma*[50] with "arms" —was the institution of legal proceedings against me which held out the grim prospect of spending many years in prison. I was forced to disappear immediately and was never again to see my home. My son was taken in by good friends, my small household liquidated. I became "an illegal." It was a time of strenuous work.

The first All-Russian Women's Congress which had been called by the bourgeois suffragettes was scheduled to take place in

43. crossed out
44. Author's correction: not so easy
45. Author's correction: comrades
46. Author's correction: Since
47. Author's correction: I
48. crossed out
49. Author's correction: and propaganda work among the masses of women-workers
50. Author's correction: Czarism

December of 1908. At that time the reaction was on the rise and the working-class movement was prostrate again after the first victory in 1905. Many Party comrades were in jail, others had fled abroad. The vehement struggle between the two factions of the Russian Workers Party broke out anew: the Bolsheviks on the one side, the Mensheviks on the other. *In 1908 I belonged to the Menshevik faction, having been forced thereto by the hostile position taken by the Bolsheviks towards the Duma, a pseudo-Parliament called by the Czar in order to pacify the rebellious spirits of the age. Along with the Mensheviks I espoused the point of view that even a pseudo-Parliament should be utilized as a tribute for our Party and that the elections for the Duma must be used as an assembling point for the working class. But I did not side with the Mensheviks on the question of coordinating the forces of the workers with the Liberals in order to accelerate the overthrow of absolutism. On this point I was, in fact, very left-radical and was even branded as a "syndicalist" by my Party comrades.*[51] Given my attitude towards the Duma it logically followed that I considered it useless to exploit the first bourgeois women's congress in the interest of our Party. Nevertheless I worked with might and main to assure that our[52] women workers, who were to participate in the Congress, emerged as an independent and distinct group. I managed to carry out this plan but not without opposition. My Party comrades[53] accused me and those women-comrades who shared my views of being "feminists" and of placing too much emphasis on matters of concern to women only. At the time there was still no compre-

51. Author's note: delete
52. Author's correction: the
53. Author's correction: (the Mensheviks)

15

hension *at all*[54] of the extraordinarily important role in the struggle devolving upon self-employed professional women. Nevertheless our will prevailed. A women-workers' group came forward at the Congress in St. Petersburg with its *own*[55] program and it drew a clear line of demarcation between the bourgeois suffragettes and the women's liberation movement of the working class in Russia. However, I was forced to flee before the close of the Congress because the police had come upon my tracks. I managed to cross the frontier into Germany and thus, in December of 1908, began a new period of my life, political emigration.

54. Author's correction: insufficient
55. Author's correction: the socialist

The Years of Political Emigration

As a political refugee henceforth I lived in Europe and America until the overthrow of Czarism in 1917. As soon as I arrived in Germany, after my flight, I joined the German Social Democratic Party in which I had many personal friends, among whom I especially numbered Karl Liebknecht,[56] Rosa Luxemburg, *Karl Kautsky*.[57] Clara Zetkin also had a great influence on my *activity*[58] in defining the principles of the women-workers movement in Russia. Already in 1907 I had taken part, as a delegate from Russia, in the first International Conference of Socialist Women that was held in Stuttgart. This gathering was presided over by Clara Zetkin and it made an enormous contribution to the development of the women-workers movement along Marxist lines. I put myself at the disposal of the Party press as a writer on social and political questions, and I was also frequently called upon as an orator by the German Party and I worked for the Party as an agitator from the Palatinate to Saxony, from Bremen to south Germany. But I assumed[59] no leading posts either in the Russian party or in the German party.[60] By and large I was mainly a "popular orator" and an esteemed political writer. *I can now openly confess*[61] that in the Russian Party I deliberately

56. Author's correction: And
57. crossed out
58. Author's correction: work
59. Author's correction: at that time I had
60. crossed out
61. crossed out

17

kept somewhat aloof from the controlling center, and that is explainable mainly by the fact that I was not yet in complete agreement with the policy of my comrades.[62] *But I had no desire to pass over to the Bolsheviks, nor could I for that matter since at the time it seemed to me as if they did not attach sufficient importance to the development of the working-class movement in "breadth and depth." Therefore I worked on my own seemingly almost as though I wanted to remain in the background without setting my sights or obtaining a leading position.*[63] Here it must be admitted that, although I possessed a certain degree of ambition, like every other active human being, I was never animated by the desire to obtain "a post." For me "what I am" was always of less importance than "what I can," that is to say, what I was in a position to accomplish. In this way I, too, had my ambition and it was especially noticeable there where I stood *with my whole heart and soul*[64] in the struggle, where the issue was the abolition of the slavery of working women. I had above all set myself the task of winning over women workers in Russia to socialism and, at the same time, of working for the liberation of[65] woman, for her equality of rights. My book "The Social Foundations of the Women's Question" had appeared shortly before my flight; it was a polemical disputation with the bourgeois suffragettes but, at the same time, a challenge to the Party to build a viable women-workers movement in Russia. The book enjoyed a great success. At that time I wrote for the legal and illegal press. Through an exchange of letters I tried to influence

62. Author's correction: (the Mensheviks)
63. Author's note: delete
64. crossed out
65. Author's correction: working

Party comrades and women workers themselves. *Naturally, I always did this in such a way that I demanded from the Party* that it[66] *espouse* the cause of women's liberation. I did not always have an easy time of it. Much passive resistance, little understanding, and even less interest for this aim, over and over again, lay as an obstacle in the path. It was not until 1914, shortly before the outbreak of the World War, that finally both factions—the Mensheviks and the Bolsheviks—took up the question in an earnest and practical way, a fact which had on me an effect almost tantamount to a personal commendation. Two periodicals for working women were launched in Russia, the International Working Women's Congress of March 8, 1914, was celebrated. I was still living in exile, however, and could help the so dearly loved women-workers movement in my homeland only from afar. I was in close contact, also from afar, with the working women of Russia. Already several years earlier[67] I had been appointed by the Textile Workers Union as an official delegate to the Second International Conference of Socialist Women (1910) and, *further*,[68] to the extraordinary International Socialist Congress in Basle in 1912. Later when a draft of a bill on social insurance was introduced in the Russian pseudo-Parliament (the Duma), the Social Democratic Duma faction (of the Menshevik wing) requested me to elaborate the draft of a bill on maternity welfare. It was not the first time that the[69] faction lay claim to my energies for legislative work. Just before I was forced to go into exile, I had been enlisted by them—as a qualified expert—to

66. Author's correction: a more zealous activity
67. crossed out
68. crossed out
69. Author's correction: Duma

19

participate in the deliberation of the question of Finland in the Imperial Duma.

The task that had been assigned to me, namely, the elaboration of a draft of a bill in the field of maternity welfare, motivated me to undertake a most thorough study of this special question. The *Bund für Mutterschutz,* and the outstanding work of Dr. Helene Stöcker, also provided me with valuable suggestions. Nevertheless I also studied the question in England, France, and in the Scandinavian countries. The result of these studies was my book "Motherhood and Society," a *comprehensive*[70] work of 600 pages on maternity welfare and the relevant legislation in Europe and Australia. The fundamental regulations and demands in this field, which I summed up at the end of my book, were realized later in 1917 by the Soviet regime in the first social insurance laws.

For me the years of political emigration were hectic, *quite stirring*[71] years. I travelled as a Party orator from country to country. In 1911, in Paris, I organized the housewives' strike "La grève des menagères" against the high cost of living. In 1912 I worked in Belgium setting the groundwork for the miners' strike in the Borinage and in the same year the Party dispatched me to the left-oriented Socialist Youth Association of Sweden in order to strengthen the Party's[72] anti-militaristic tendencies. Several years earlier, *this still merits mention here,*[73] I fought in the ranks of the British Socialist Party side by side with Dora Montefiore *and Madame Koeltsch*[74] against the English suffragettes for the strengthening of the still fledgling socialist working-

70. Author's correction: a
71. crossed out
72. Author's correction: in Sweden
73. crossed out
74. crossed out

women's movement. In 1913 I was again in England. This time I was there in order to take an active part in a protest action against the famous "Beilis Trial" which had been instigated by the anti-semites in Russia. In the spring of the same year, the left wing of the Swedish Social Democratic Party invited me to Sweden. These were truly hectic years, marked by the most varied types of militant activity. Notwithstanding, my Russian Party comrades also laid claim to my energies and appointed me delegate to the Socialist Party and Trade Union Congress. *Thus with the help of Karl Liebknecht I also sparked an activity in Germany on behalf of the deported socialist members of the Duma.*[75] In 1911 I was called to the Russian Party School in Bologna, where I delivered a series of lectures. The present Russian Minister of Education in Soviet Russia, A. Lunacharsky, Maxim Gorki, as well as the famous Russian economist and philosopher A. Bogdonov, were the founders of this Party school, and Trotsky delivered lectures at the school at the same time that I was there. The present Soviet Russian Minister of Foreign Affairs, G. Chicherin, who at that time worked as secretary of a relief agency for political refugees, oftentimes called upon me to hold public lectures on the most disparate cultural problems of Russian life in order to help fill the relief agency's almost empty kitty. At his behest I travelled all over Europe but Berlin was my fixed abode. I felt at home in Germany and have always greatly appreciated the conditions there so ideally suited for scientific work. But I was not allowed to give speeches in Prussia. On the contrary, I had to keep as quiet as possible to avoid expulsion by the Prussian police.

75. Author's note: delete

Then the World War broke out and once again I arrived at a new turning point in my life.

But before I talk about this important period of my intellectual existence, I still want to say a few words about my personal life. The question rises whether in the middle of all these manifold, exciting labors and Party-assignments I could still find time for intimate experiences, for the pangs and joys of love. Unfortunately, yes! I say unfortunately because ordinarily these experiences entailed all too many cares, disappointments, and pain, and because all too many energies were pointlessly consumed through them. Yet the longing to be understood by a man down to the deepest, most secret recesses of one's soul, to be recognized by him as a striving human being, repeatedly decided matters. And repeatedly disappointment ensued all too swiftly, since the friend saw in me only the feminine element which he tried to mold into a willing sounding board to his own ego. So repeatedly the moment inevitably arrived in which I had to shake off the chains of community with an aching heart but with a sovereign, uninfluenced will. Then I was again alone. But the greater the demands life made upon me, the more the responsible work waiting to be tackled, the greater grew the longing to be enveloped by love, warmth, understanding. All the easier, consequently, began the old story of disappointment in love, the old story of Titania in "A Midsummer Night's Dream."[76]

The outbreak of the World War found me in Germany. My son was with me. We were both arrested because my identity papers were not in order. During the house search, however, the police found a mandate from the Russian Social Democratic Party appointing me as delegate to the World Congress of

76. Author's note: delete

Socialists. Suddenly the gentlemen from Alexander Platz became utterly charming: they figured that a female Social Democrat could not be a friend of the Czar *and consequently certainly not an enemy of Germany. They were right.*[77] I was in fact no enemy of Germany and still less a Russian patriot. To me the war was an abomination, a madness, a crime, and from the first moment onwards—more out of impulse than reflection—I inwardly rejected it and could never reconcile myself with it *up to this very moment.*[78] The intoxication of patriotic feelings has always been something alien to me, on the contrary I felt an aversion for everything that smacked of super-patriotism. I found no understanding for my "anti-patriotic" attitude among my own *Russian*[79] Party comrades, *who also lived in Germany.*[80] Only Karl Liebknecht, his wife Sofie Liebknecht, and a few other German Party comrades, like myself, espoused the same standpoint and, *like myself,*[18] considered it a socialist's duty to struggle against the war. Strange to say, I was present in the Reichstag on August 4, the day the war budget was being voted on. The collapse of the German Socialist Party struck me as a calamity without parallel. I felt utterly alone and found comfort only in the company of the Liebknechts.

With the help of some German Party friends I was able to leave Germany with my son in August of 1914 and emigrate to the Scandinavian peninsula. I left Germany not because I had felt the slightest manifestation of unfriendliness towards me but only

77. crossed out
78. crossed out
79. crossed out
80. Author's correction: at that time
81. crossed out

for the reason that without a sphere of activity I would have been forced to live in idleness in that country. I was impatient to take up the struggle against the war. After arriving on Sweden's neutral soil, I *immediately*[82] began the work against the war *and for*[83] *the* international solidarity of the world working class. An appeal to working women made its way, along illegal channels, to Russia and to different other countries. In Sweden I wrote and spoke against the war. I spoke at public meetings, most of which had been called by the leftist-leaning *world-famous*[84] Swedish Party leaders Zeta Höglund and Frederic Strön. I found in them the pure echo of my *ideas and*[85] feelings and we joined forces in a common task for the victory of internationalism and against the war hysteria. It was only later that I learned of the attitude which the leading minds of the Russian Party had taken towards the war. When the news finally reached us, by way of Paris and Switzerland, it was for us a day of ineffable joy. We received assurance that both Trotsky and Lenin, although they[86] belonged to different factions of the Party, had militantly risen up against the war. Thus I was no longer "isolated." *A new grouping was proposed*[87] in the Party, the internationalists and the "social-patriots." *A Party periodical was also founded in Paris.*[88] In the middle of my zealous activities, however, I was arrested by the Swedish authorities and brought to the Kungsholm prison. The worst moment during this arrest was born of my concern over the

82. crossed out
83. Author's correction: through revival of the
84. crossed out
85. crossed out
86. Author's correction: both
87. Author's correction: a new grouping took place
88. crossed out

identity papers of a good friend and Party comrade, Alexander Schlapnikov, who had just arrived illegally in Sweden from Russia, which I had taken over for safe-keeping. Under the eyes of the police I managed to hide them under my blouse and somehow make them disappear. Later I was transferred from the Kungsholm prison to the prison in Malmö and then banished to Denmark. As far as I know I was one of the first of the European socialists to be jailed because of anti-war propaganda. In Denmark *I continued my work but with greater prudence. Nevertheless*[89] the Danish police did not leave me in peace. Nor did the Danish Social Democrats exhibit friendliness for the internationalists. In February of 1915 I emigrated to Norway where together with Alexander Schlapnikov we served as a link between Switzerland, the place of residence of Lenin and of the Central Committee,[90] and Russia. We had full contact with the Norwegian socialists. On March 8 of the same year I tried to organize an international working women's demonstration against the war in Christiania (now Oslo), but the representatives from the belligerent countries did not show up.

That was the time when the decisive rupture in Social Democracy was being prepared, since the patriotically minded socialists could not go along with the internationalists. Since the Bolsheviks were those who most consistently fought social-patriotism, in June of 1915 I officially joined the Bolsheviks *and entered into a lively correspondence with Lenin (Lenin's letters to me have recently been published in Russia).*[91]

I again began to do a prodigous amount of writing, this time

89. crossed out
90. Author's correction: of our Party
91. crossed out

25

for the international-minded press of the most different countries: England, Norway, Sweden, America, Russia. At this time one of my pamphlets, "Who Profits from the War?," appeared. Deliberately written in a very popular view, it was disseminated in countless editions, *in millions of copies*,[92] and was translated into several languages, German included. So long as the war continued, the problem of women's liberation obviously had to recede into the background since *my only concern, my highest aim*,[93] was to fight against the war and call a new Workers International into being. In the autumn of 1915 the German section of the American Socialist Party invited me to journey to America to deliver lectures there in the spirit of "Zimmerwald" (a gathering of international-minded socialists). I was immediately ready to cross the ocean for this purpose, despite the fact that my friends determinedly advised me against it. They were all deeply worried about me because the journey had become very hazardous as a result of submarine warfare. But the aim enticed me enormously. My propaganda tour in America lasted five months, during which time *I visited eighty-one cities in the United States and delivered lectures in German, French, and Russian*.[94] The work was extremely strenuous, *but also as fruitful, and I had warrant to believe that as a result the internationalists in the American Party were strengthened. Much opposition to the war, passionate debates, also existed overseas, but the police did not bother me*.[95] The newspapers, by turns, branded me either

92. crossed out
93. Author's correction: our only and living aim
94. Author's correction: I had to cross the whole of the United States from the Atlantic to the Pacific Ocean and deliver lectures in the most different languages along the lines of the Internationalists
95. Author's note: delete

as a spy of the German Kaiser or as an agent of the Entente. I returned to Norway in the spring of 1916. I love Norway with its incomparable fjords and its majestic mountains, its courageous, gifted, and industrious people. At that time I lived on the famous Holmenkollen near Oslo and continued to work with the view of welding together all the forces of the internationalists in opposition to the World War. *I shared Lenin's view which aimed at spreading the conviction that the war could be defeated only by the Revolution, by the uprising of the workers. I was in substantial agreement with Lenin and stood much closer to him than many of his older followers and friends.*[96] But my sojourn in Norway was not a long one because only a few months after my arrival I had to embark upon a second journey to America, where I remained till shortly before the outbreak of the Russian Revolution. *For me the situation in America had changed insofar as, in the meanwhile, many Russian Party comrades had come over, Trotsky among others. We worked zealously for the new Workers International but America's intervention in the war aggravated our activity.*[97]

I had already been in Norway for several weeks, when the Russian people rose up against absolutism and dethroned the Czar. A festive mood reigned among all our political friends. But I harbored no illusions because I knew that the overthrow of the Czar would be only the beginning of even more momentous events and difficult social struggles *so I hastened*[98] back to Russia in March 1917. I was one of the first political emigrants *who*

96. Author's note: delete
97. Author's note: delete
98. Author's correction: as soon as the political amnesty was declared by the new Republic I hastened
99. Author's correction: who had the luck to

came[99] back to the liberated homeland. Torneo, the tiny frontier town lying north of the Swedish-Finnish frontiers, through which I had to pass, was still in the grip of a cruel winter. A sleigh carried me across the river which marks the frontier. On Russian soil stood a soldier. A bright red ribbon fluttered on his chest. "Your identity papers, please, citizenness!" "I have none. I am a political refugee." "Your name?" I identified myself. A young officer was summoned. Yes, my name was on the list of political refugees who were to be freely admitted into the country by order of the Workers' and Soldiers' Soviet. The young officer helped me out of the sleigh and kissed my hand, almost reverently. I was standing on the republican soil of liberated Russia! Could that be possible? It was one of the happiest hours of my *whole*[100] life. Four months later, by order of the Kerensky regime (the Provisional Government), the same charming young officer placed me under arrest as a dangerous Bolshevik at the Torneo frontier station . . . Such is life's irony.

100. crossed out

The Years of Revolution

So overwhelming was the rush of subsequent events that to this very day I really do not know what I should describe and emphasize: what have I accomplished, desired, achieved? Was there altogether an individual will at that time? Was it not only the omnipotent storm of the Revolution, the command of the active, awakened masses that determined our will and action? Was there altogether a single human being who would not have bowed to the general will? There were only masses of people, bound together in a bipartite will, which operated either for or against the Revolution, for or against ending the war, and which sided for or against the power of the Soviets. Looking back one perceives only a massive operation, struggle, and action. In reality there were no heroes or leaders. It was the people, the working people, in soldiers' uniform or in civilian attire, who controlled the situation and who recorded its will indelibly in the history of the country and mankind. It was a sultry summer, a crucial summer of the revolutionary flood-tide in 1917! At first the social storm raged only in the countryside, the peasants set fire to the "nests of gentle folk." In the cities the struggle that raged was between the advocates of a republican-bourgeois Russia and the socialist aspirations of the Bolsheviks . . .

As I have previously stated, I belonged to the Bolsheviks. Thus immediately, from the first days onwards, I found an absolute enormous pile of work waiting for me. Once more the issue was to wage a struggle against the war, against coalescence with the liberal bourgeoisie, and for the power of the workers' councils, the Soviets. The natural consequence of this stand was that the bourgeois newspapers branded me as a "mad female Bolshevik." But this bothered me not at all. *My field of activity was immense, and my followers, factory workers and women-soldiers, numbered thousands.*[101] At this time I was very popular, especially[102] as an orator,[103] and, at the same time, hated and viciously attacked by the bourgeois press. *Thus it was a stroke of luck that I was*[104] so weighed down with current work that I found hardly any time to read the attacks and slanders against me. The hate directed against me, allegedly because I had been in the pay of the German Kaiser for the purpose of weakening the Russian front, grew[105] to monstrous proportions.

One of the most burning questions of the day was the high cost of living and the growing scarcity of vital necessities. Thus the women of the poverty-stricken strata had an indescribably hard time of it. *Precisely this situation prepared the terrain in the Party for "work with women" so that very soon we were able to accomplish useful work.*[106] Already in May of 1917 a weekly called "The Women Workers" made its debut. *I authored an appeal to women against the high cost of living and the war.*[107] The first

101. Author's note: delete
102. crossed out
103. Author's correction: with the workers, the soldiers, the working women and the women soldiers
104. Author's correction: I, however, was
105. Author's correction: grew among the non-Soviet minded strata
106. Author's correction: This gave our Party occasion to initiate enlightenment and political work among working women
107. crossed out

mass meeting, packed with thousands of people,[108] that took place in Russia under the Provisional Government, was organized by us, by the Bolsheviks. Kerensky and his ministers made no secret of their hatred of me, the "instigator of the spirit of dis-organization" in the Army. One particular article of mine in "Pravda" in which I interceded for German prisoners of war unleashed *a veritable storm of*[109] indignation on the part of patriotic-minded circles. When in April Lenin delivered his famous programmatic speech within the frame of the Soviets, *I was the only one of his Party comrades who took the floor to support his theses. What hatred this particular act kindled against me!*[110] Often I had to jump off tramcars before people recognized me, since I had become a topical theme of the day and often bore personal witness to the most incredible abuse and lies directed against me. *I should like to cite a small example which can show how the enemy worked with might and main to defame me. At that time the newspapers hostile to me were already writing about the "Kollontai party dresses" which particularly then was laughable because my trunk had been lost en route to Russia, so I always wore the one and the same dress. There was even a little street ballad that commented on Lenin and me in verse.*[111] There was also nothing extraordinary in the fact that, threatened as I was by irritated mobs, I was always protected from the worst only by the courageous intercession of my friends and Party comrades. Nevertheless I myself personally *experienced little*[112] of the hatred

108. Author's correction: under the slogan of international solidarity and against the war
109. Author's correction: the
110. Author's note: delete
111. Author's note: delete
112. Author's correction: did not worry at all

31

around me and, of course, there was also a great number of enthusiastic friends: the workers, the sailors, the soldiers *who were utterly devoted to me*.[113] Moreover, the number *of our followers*[114] grew from day to day. Already in April, I was a member of the Soviet executive which, in reality, was the guiding political body of the moment, to which I belonged as the only woman and over a long period. In May of 1917 I took part in the strike of women laundry workers who set forth the demand that all laundries be "municipalized." The struggle lasted six weeks. Nevertheless the principal demand of the women laundry workers remained unmet by the Kerensky regime.

At the end of June, I was sent by my Party to Stockholm as a delegate to an international consultation which was interrupted when news reached us of the July uprising against the Provisional Government and of the extremely harsh measures that the[115] government was taking against the Bolsheviks. Many of our leading Party comrades had already been arrested, others, including Lenin, had managed to escape and go into hiding. The Bolsheviks were accused of high treason and branded as spies of the German Kaiser. The uprising was brought to a standstill and the coalition regime retaliated against all those who had manifested sympathy for the Bolsheviks. I immediately decided to return to Russia, although my friends *and Party comrades*[116] considered this to be a risky undertaking. They wanted me to go to Sweden and await the course of events. Well-intentioned as these counsels were, *and correct as they also appeared to me*

113. crossed out
114. Author's correction: of the Bolsheviks
115. Author's correction: Provisional (Kerensky)
116. crossed out

later,[117] I nevertheless could not heed them. I simply had to go back. Otherwise it would appear to me as an act of cowardice to take advantage of the privilege, that had become mine, of remaining wholly immune from the persecutions of the Provisional Government, when a great number of my political friends were sitting in jail. *Later I realized that, perhaps, I might have been able to be more useful to our cause from Sweden, but I was under the compulsion of the moment.*[118] By order of the Kerensky regime I was arrested on the border of Torneo and subjected to the most boorish treatment as a spy . . . But the arrest itself proceeded quite theatrically: during the inspection of my passport I was requested to step into the commandant's office. I understood what that meant. A number of soldiers were standing in an enormous room, pressed close against each other. Two young officers were also present, one of them being the charming young man who had received me *so amiably*[119] four months previously. A *veritable*[120] silence prevailed in the room. The facial expression of the first officer, Prince B., betrayed a great nervousness. Composed, I waited to see what would happen next. "You are under arrest," explained Prince B. "So. Has the counter-revolution triumphed? Do we again have a monarchy?" "No," was the gruff reply. "You are under arrest by order of the Provisional Government." "I have been expecting it. Please, let my suitcase be brought in, I don't want it to be lost." "But, of course. Lieutenant, the suitcase!" I saw how the officers heaved a sigh of relief, and how the soldiers left the room with displeasure writ

117. crossed out
118. crossed out
119. Author's correction: amicably
120. Author's correction: strange

33

large on their faces. Later I learned that my arrest had occasioned a protest among the soldiers who insisted upon witnessing the arrest. The officers, however, had feared that I might make a speech to the soldiers. "In that case we would have been lost," one of them told me afterwards.

I was forced to wait for the course of the investigation, like the other Bolsheviks, in a Petrograd prison, in strict isolation. The more incredibly the regime conducted itself towards the Bolsheviks, the more *their* influence grew.[121] The march of the White general Kornilov on Petrograd strengthened the most radical elements of the Revolution. The people demanded that the jailed Bolsheviks be freed. Kerensky, however, refused to free me and it was only by an order of the Soviet that I was released from jail upon payment of bail. But already on the next day, Kerensky's decree that I be placed under house arrest hung over me. Nevertheless I was given my full freedom of movement one month before the decisive struggle, the October Revolution in 1917. Again my work piled up. Now the groundwork was to be set for a systematic women-workers movement. The first conference of women workers was to be called. It also took place and it coincided with the overthrow of the Provisional Government and the establishment of the Soviet Republic.

At that time I was a member of the highest Party body, the Central Committee, *and I voted for the policy of armed uprising.*[122] I was also a member of different Party representations in decisive Congresses and State institutions (the preliminary Parliament, the democratic Congress, etc.). Then came the great days of the October Revolution. Smolny became historic. The

121. Author's correction: of Bolshevism
122. Author's correction: crossed out

34

sleepless nights, the permanent sessions. And, finally, the stirring declarations. "The Soviets take power!" "The Soviets address an appeal to the peoples of the world to put an end to the war." "The land is socialized and belongs to the peasants!"

The Soviet Government was formed. I was appointed People's Commissar (Minister) of Social Welfare. I was the only woman in the cabinet *and the first woman in history*[123] who had ever been recognized as a member of a government. When one recalls the first months of the Workers' Government, months which were so rich in *magnificent illusions,*[124] plans,[125] ardent initiatives to improve life, to organize the world anew, months of the real romanticism of the Revolution, one would in fact like to write about all else save about one's self. I occupied the post of Minister of Social Welfare from October of 1917 *to March of 1918.*[126] It was not without opposition that I was received by the former officials of the Ministry. Most of them sabotaged us openly and simply did not show up for work. But precisely this office could not interrupt its work, come what may, since in itself it was an extraordinarily complicated operation. It included the whole welfare program for the war-disabled, hence for hundreds of thousands of crippled soldiers and officers, the pension system in general, foundling homes, homes for the aged, orphanages, hospitals for the needy, the work-shops making artificial limbs, the administration of playing-card factories (the manufacture of playing cards was a State monopoly), *the educational system,*[127]

123. Author's correction: So far as I knew it was the first time in history that a woman
124. Author's correction: great aims and
125. Author's correction: in
126. crossed out
127. Author's correction: leper colonies

clinical hospitals for women.[128] In addition a whole series of educational institutes for young girls were also under the direction of this Ministry. One can easily imagine the enormous demands these tasks made upon a small group of people who, at the same time, were novices in State administration. In a clear awareness of these difficulties *I formed,*[129] immediately, an auxiliary council in which experts such as physicians, jurists, pedagogues were represented alongside the workers and the minor officials of the Ministry. The sacrifice, the energy with which the minor employees bore the burden of this difficult task was truly exemplary. It was not only a matter of keeping the work of the Ministry going, but also of initiating reforms and improvements. New, fresh forces replaced the sabotaging officers of the old regime. A new life stirred in the offices of the formerly highly conservative Ministry. Days of grueling work! And at night the sessions of the councils of the People's Commissar (of the cabinet) under Lenin's chairmanship. A small, modest room and only one secretary who recorded the resolutions which changed Russia's life to its bottommost foundations. *My first act*[130] as People's Commissar *was*[131] to compensate a small peasant for his requisitioned horse. Actually by no stretch of the imagination did this belong to the functions of my office. But the man was determined to receive compensation for his horse. He had travelled from his distant village to the capital and had knocked patiently on the doors of all the ministries. Always with no results! Then the Bolshevik revolution broke out. The man had

128. Author's correction: etc.
129. Author's correction: we formed
130. Author's correction: my first day
131. Author's correction: began as follows

heard that the Bolsheviks were in favor of the workers and peasants. So he went to the Smolny Institute, to Lenin, who had to pay out the compensation. I do not know how the conversation between Lenin and the small peasant went. As a result of it, however, the man came to me with a small page torn from Lenin's notebook on which I was requested to settle the matter somehow since at the moment the People's Commissariat for Social Welfare had the greatest amount of cash at its disposal. The small peasant received his compensation.

My main work as People's Commissar consisted in the following:[132] by decree to improve the situation of the war-disabled, to abolish religious instruction in the schools for young girls which were under the Ministry (this was still before the general separation of Church and State), and to transfer priests to the civil service, to introduce the right of self-administration for pupils in the schools for girls, to reorganize the former orphanages into government Children's Homes (*no distinction was to be made between orphaned children and those who still had fathers and mothers*),[133] to set up the first hostels for the needy and street-urchins, to convene a committee, composed *only*[134] of doctors, which was to be commissioned *to elaborate*[135] the free public health system for the whole country. In my opinion the most important accomplishment of the People's Commissariat, however, was the legal foundation of a Central Office for Maternity and Infant Welfare. The draft of the bill relating to this

132. Author's correction: the most important achievements of our Peoples Commissariat (Ministry for Social Welfare) in the first months after the October Revolution were the following:
133. crossed out
134. crossed out
135. Author's correction: to work out

37

Central Office was signed by me in January of 1918. A second decree followed in which I[136] changed all maternity hospitals into free Homes for Maternity and Infant Care,[137] in order thereby to set the groundwork for a comprehensive government system of pre-natal care. I was greatly assisted in coping with these tasks by Dr. Korolef. We also planned a "Pre-Natal Care Palace," a model home with an exhibition room in which courses for mothers would be held *and, among many other things,*[138] model day nurseries were also to be established.[139] We were just about completing preparations for such a facility in the building of a girls' boarding school at which formerly young girls of the nobility had been educated and which was still under the direction of a countess, when a fire destroyed our work, which had barely begun! Had the fire been set deliberately? . . . I was dragged out of bed in the middle of the night. I rushed to the scene of the fire; the beautiful exhibition room was totally ruined, as were all the other rooms. Only the huge name-plate "Pre-Natal Care Palace" still hung over the entrance door.

My efforts to nationalize maternity and infant care set off a new wave of insane attacks against me. All kinds of lies were related[140] about the "nationalization of women," *about my legislative proposals which assertedly ordained that little girls of 12 were to become mothers.* A special fury gripped the religious

136. crossed out
137. Author's correction: were
138. crossed out
139. Author's correction: etc.
140. Author's correction: written in Russian, on laws which "obligated" 12-year old girls to become mothers and suchlike

followers of the old regime when, *on my own authority* (*the cabinet later criticized me for this action*),[141] I transformed the famous Alexander Nevsky monastery into a home for war-invalids. The monks resisted and a shooting fray ensued. The press again raised a loud hue and cry against *me*.[142] The Church organized street demonstrations *against my action*[143] and also pronounced "anathema' against me . . .

I received countless threatening letters, but I never requested military protection. I always went out alone, unarmed and without any kind of a bodyguard. In fact I never gave a thought to any kind of danger, being all too engrossed in matters of an utterly different character.[144] In February of 1918 a first State delegation of the Soviets was sent to Sweden *in order to clarify different economic and political questions.*[145] As Peoples' Commissar I headed this delegation. But our vessel was shipwrecked; we were saved by landing on the Aland Islands which belonged to Finland. At this very time the struggle between the Whites and the Reds in the country had reached its most crucial moment and the German Army was also making ready to wage war against Finland.

The White troops occupied the Aland Islands on the very evening of our shipwreck as we were seated at dinner in an inn of the city of Marieham, rejoicing over our rescue. We managed to escape thanks to the greatest determination and cunning, yet

141. Author's correction: we
142. Author's correction: our action
143. crossed out
144. Author's note: delete
145. crossed out

one of our group, a young[146] Finn, was captured and shot. We returned to Petrograd, where the evacuation of the capital was being prepared with feverish haste: German troops already stood before the gates of the city.

Now began a *dark time*[147] of my life which I cannot treat of here since the events are still too fresh in my mind. *But the day will also come when I will give an account of them.*[148]

There were differences of opinion in the Party. I resigned from my post as People's Commissar *on the ground of total disagreement with the current policy. Little by little I was also relieved of all my other tasks. I again gave lectures and espoused my ideas on "the new woman" and "the new morality."*[150] The Revolution was in full swing. The struggle was becoming increasingly irreconcilable and bloodier, *much of what was happening did not fit in with my outlook.*[151] But after all[152] there was still the unfinished task, women's liberation. Women, of course, had received all rights but in practice, of course, they still lived under the old yoke: without authority in family life, enslaved by a thousand menial household chores, bearing the whole burden of maternity, even the material cares, because many women now found life alone as a result of the war and other circumstances.

In the autumn of 1916 when I devoted all my energies to drawing up systematic guidelines for the liberation of working women

146. Author's correction: "red" (in quotes)
147. Author's correction: period
148. crossed out
149. crossed out: Author's correction: I
150. Author's note: delete
151. crossed out
152. Author's correction: also

in all areas, *I found a valuable support in the*[153] first President of the Soviets, Sverdlov, now dead.[154] Thus the first Congress of Women Workers and Women Peasants could be called as early as November of 1918; some 1147 delegates were present. Thus the foundation was laid for methodical work in the whole country for the *liberation*[155] of the women of the working and the peasant classes. A flood of new work was waiting for me. The question now was one of drawing women into the people's kitchens and of educating them to devote their energies to children's homes and day-care centers, the school system, household reforms, and still many other pressing matters. The main thrust of all this activity was to implement, in fact, equal rights for women as a labor unit in the national economy and as a citizen in the political sphere and, of course, with the special proviso: maternity was to be appraised as a social function and therefore protected and provided for by the State.

Under the guidance of Dr. Lebedevo, the State institutes for pre-natal care also flourished then. At the same time, central officers were established in the whole country to deal with issues and tasks connected with women's liberation and to draw women into Soviet work.

The Civil War in 1919 saddled me with new tasks. When the White troops tried to march north from south Russia, I was again sent to the Ukraine and to the Crimea where at first I served as

153. Author's correction: it was the
154. Author's correction: who recognized the task of the political education of working women as a serious aim of the Party and helped us in our work
155. Author's correction: emancipation
156. Author's correction: to win them over to the new political system, to educate them politically

chairwoman of the enlightenment department in the Army. Later, *up to the evacuation of the Soviet government,*[157] I was appointed People's Commissar of Enlightenment and Propaganda in the Ukrainian government. *I managed to send 400 women communists out of the threatened zone near Kiev with a special train. I did my most possible best for the communist women-workers movement also in the Ukraine.*[158]

A serious illness tore me away from the exciting work for months. Hardly having recovered—at that time I was in Moscow —I took over the direction of the Coordinating Office for Work among Women and again a new period of intensive, grueling work began. A communist women's *newspaper*[159] was founded, conferences and congresses of women workers were convoked. The foundation was laid for work with the women of the East (Mohammedans). Two world conferences of communist women took place in Moscow. The law liberalizing abortion was put through and a number of regulations of benefit to women were introduced by our Coordinating Office and legally confirmed. *At this time I had to do more writing and speaking than ever before . . .*[160] Our work received wholehearted support from Lenin. And Trotsky, although he was overburdened with military tasks, unfailingly and gladly appeared at our conferences. Energetic, gifted women, two of whom are no longer alive,[161] sacrificially devoted all their energies to the work of the Coordinating Office.

At the eighth Soviet Congress, as a member of the Soviet execu-

157. crossed out
158. Author's note: delete
159. Author's correction: periodical
160. crossed out
161. Author's correction: Inessa Armand, and Samoslova

tive (*now there were already several women on this body*[162]), I proposed a motion that the Soviets in all areas contribute to the creation of a consciousness of the struggle for equal rights for women and, accordingly, to involve them in State and communal work. I[163] managed to push the motion through and to get it accepted but not without resistance. It was a great, an enduring victory.

A heated debate flared up when I published my thesis on the new morality. *For our Soviet marriage law, separated from the Church to be sure, is not essentially more progressive than the same laws that after all exist in other progressive democratic countries. Marriage, civil marriage and*[164] although the illegitimate child *was*[165] placed on a legal par with the legitimate child,[166] in practice a great deal of hypocrisy and injustice still exists in this area. When one speaks of the "immorality" which the Bolsheviks purportedly propagated, it suffices to submit our marriage laws to a close scrutiny to note that in the divorce question we are on a par with North America whereas in the question of the illegitimate child we have *not yet even*[167] progressed as far as the Norwegians.

The most radical wing of the Party was formed around this question. My theses, my *sexual and moral*[168] views,[169] were bitterly fought *by many Party comrades of both sexes:*[170] *as were*

162. crossed out
163. Author's correction: we
164. crossed out
165. Author's correction: in Soviet Russia
166. Author's correction: is
167. Author's correction: only
168. crossed out
169. Author's correction: in the area of sexual morality
170. crossed out

43

still other differences of opinion in the Party regarding political guiding principles.[171] Personal and family cares were added thereto and thus months in 1922 went by without fruitful work. Then in the autumn of 1922 came my official appointment to the legation of the Russian Soviet representation in Norway. I really believed that this appointment would be purely formal and that therefore in Norway I would find time to devote to myself, to my literary activity. Things turned out quite differently. With the day of my entry into office in Norway I also entered upon a wholly new course of work in my life which drew upon all my energies to the highest degree. During my diplomatic activity, therefore, I *wrote only one article, "The Winged Eros," which caused an extraordinarily great flutter. Added to this were three short novels, "Paths of Love," which have been published by Malik-Verlag in Berlin.*[172] My book "The New Morality and the Working Class" and a socio-economic study, "The Condition of Women in the Evolution of Political Economy," were written when I was still in Russia.

171. crossed out

172. Author's correction: wrote little: three short stories, "Paths of Love," my first attempt at short-story writing, a sociological article "Winged Eros," and other unimportant articles.

The Years of Diplomatic Service

I took up my duties in Norway in October of 1922 and as early as 1923 the head of the legation went on holiday so that I had officially to conduct the affairs of the Soviet Republic for him. Soon thereafter, however, I was appointed as the representative of my country in his stead. Naturally this appointment created a great sensation since, after all, it was the first time in history that a woman was officially active as an "ambassador." The conservative press and especially the Russian "White" press were outraged and tried to make a real monster of immorality and a bloody bogy out of me. Now especially a profusion of articles were written *about my "horrid views" in relation to marriage and love.* Nevertheless I must stress here *that it was only the conservative press that gave me such an unfriendly reception in my new position. In*[173] all the social relations which I had during the three[174] years of my *work*[175] in Norway, I never once experienced the least trace of aversion or mistrust against woman's capabilities. To be sure, the healthy, democratic spirit of the Norwegian people greatly contributed to this. Thus the fact is to be confirmed that my work as official *Russian*[176] representative[177] in Norway was never, and in no wise, made difficult for the reason that I

173. Author's correction: that in
174. Author's correction: and one half
175. Author's correction: diplomatic activity
176. crossed out
177. Author's correction: the Soviet Republic

belonged "to the weaker sex." In connection with my position as ambassadress I also had to assume the duties of a Trade Plenipotentiary of the Russian governmental trade representation in Norway. Naturally both tasks in their special way were new to me. *Nevertheless I set myself the*[178] *task of effecting the de jure* recognition of Soviet Russia and of re-establishing normal trade relations between the two countries which had been broken by the war and the revolution.[179] The work began with great zeal and the most roseate hopes. A *splendid*[180] summer and an eventful winter marked the year of 1923! The newly resumed trade relations were in full swing: Russian corn and Norwegian herring and fish, Russian wood products and Norwegian paper and cellulose. On February 15, 1924, Norway in fact[181] recognized the U.S.S.R. de jure. I was appointed "chargé d'affaires" and officially introduced into the diplomatic corps. Now negotiations for a trade treaty between the two countries began. My life was as crammed with strenuous work and highly interesting experiences alike. *I*[182] had also to settle grave questions connected with the further development of trade and of shipping. After several months, in August of 1924, I was appointed "Ministre Plenipotentiere" and handed over my warrant to the king of Norway with the usual ceremonial. This, of course, gave the conservative press of all countries another occasion to spew their invectives upon me. After all, never before in all history had a woman been accepted as ambassador with the customary pomp and ceremony.

178. Author's correction: The
179. Author's correction: laid special claim on my energies
180. Author's correction: laden with work
181. Author's correction: (in fact) [in parentheses]
182. Author's correction: we

The trade agreement was concluded *in Moscow*[183] at the end of 1925 and in February *I countersigned the ratified treaty in Oslo with the president of the Norwegian cabinet, I. L. Mowickl.*[184]

The signing marked the successful accomplishment of my whole mission in Norway. I could hasten towards new goals and *for this reason*[185] I left my post in Norway.

If I have attained something in this world, it was not my personal qualities that originally brought this about. Rather my achievements are only a symbol of the fact that woman, after all, is already on the march to general recognition. It is the drawing of millions of women into productive work, which was swiftly effected especially during the war and which thrust into the realm of possibility the fact that a woman could be advanced to the highest political and diplomatic positions. Nevertheless it is obvious that only a country of the future, such as the Soviet Union, can dare to confront woman without any prejudice, to appraise her only from the standpoint of her skills and talents, and, accordingly, to entrust her with responsible tasks. Only the fresh revolutionary storms were strong enough to sweep away hoary prejudices against woman and only the productive-working people is able to effect the complete equalization and liberation of woman by building a new society.

As I now end this autobiography, I stand on the threshold of new missions and life is making new demands upon me ...

No matter what further tasks I shall be carrying out, it is perfectly clear to me that the complete liberation of the working

183. crossed out
184. Author's correction: the trade agreement was ratified
185. crossed out
186. Author's correction: and to be sent to Mexico as ambassadress of the Soviet Union

woman and the creation of the foundation of a new sexual morality will always remain the highest aim of my activity, and of my life.[187]

In July of 1926

Signed: Alexandra Kollontai

187. Author's note: delete

THE NEW WOMAN

Part One

What—the new woman? Does she really exist? Is she not the product of the creative fancy of modern writers of fiction, in search of sensational novelties? Look around you, look sharply, reflect, and you will convince yourself: the new woman is certainly there—she exists.

You already know her, you are already accustomed to meeting her in life, and indeed on all rungs of the social ladder, from the woman worker up to the young women adepts of the sciences, from the modest woman clerk to the most famous representative of the liberal arts. What is most amazing about all this is that although you meet the new woman in life with ever increasing frequency, it is only in most recent years that you have had an opportunity to find her facial features more frequently again in the heroines of literary works. Life in the last decades, under the heavy hammer blows of vital necessity, has forged a woman with a new psychological sense, new needs, and a new temper. But literature still portrayed the woman of the past, still created the decrepit, self-sublimating former type. What shining images of the nascent "new woman" was offered by the reality of Russian life in the '70's and '80's! But the poets and novelists passed them by. They neither perceived nor heard them, nor did they comprehend them or distinguish among them. Turgenev almost brought them to life with his delicate brush, but even in his novels the images are dimmer, poorer than the reality. Only in his poetry, in poems in prose that are dedicated to the Russiar girl, did Turgenev bare his head reverently before the deeply affecting images of those who had dared to cross the hallowed threshold.

A long train of "nameless" ones follows the women militants, namely, those who are listed in the annals of history. They were destroyed like bees in the destroyed beehive. The rocky path to the holy, longed for, and awaited future is strewn with their corpses. Their number grew, increased year to year. But the novelists and the poets passed them by, thickly blindfolded. The poet's eye, as though it were absolutely oriented upon the traditional view of woman, was not able to grasp this *novum*, to appropriate it and stamp it upon his memory. Literature, in perfecting itself, developing by seeking utterly new paths, new colors and worlds, stubbornly continued to produce the betrayed, abandoned, suffering creatures, revengeful wives, bewitching predators, will-less "misunderstood natures," pure, colorless, charming girls.

Flaubert wrote *Madame Bovary* at a time when George Sand, so shining a herald of the new woman awakening to life, lived near him in flesh and blood, suffering and asserting her human and feminine "ego" alike.

Tolstoy immersed himself in the feminine psyche, enslaved through the centuries by fate, of an Anna Karenina. He admired a charming, harmless Kitti, toyed with the temperamental "wifie" nature of a Natasha Rostov at a time when a pitiless reality tied the hands of an ever growing, steadily increasing number of female human beings. Even the greatest talents of the nineteenth century did not feel the necessity to replace the glamor of the womanliness of their heroines by characteristics pointing to the new woman. It is only in the last ten to fifteen years that this type, newly awakened to life, has not gone unnoticed—and, of course, only by the most modern writers and especially by women novelists—as a result of which they had no choice but to assert their claim to recognition in their most recent works. Now, this type no longer presents a sensational novelty. You meet it not only in a "pioneering" novel that tries to solve one of the pressing, complicated problems of our times, as an exemplary case, but you run across it also in the modest, unpretentious narrative.

It goes without saying that the type of the "new woman" varies from country to country, that membership in this or that social stratum gives it its particular stamp, that the psychological expression of the heroine, her strivings, her life-goals, can exhibit a significant divergence from each other. But no matter how different these new heroines may be, we perceive in them something that is common to all of them, something "species-like," so to speak, which immediately enables us to distinguish them from the women of the past. The latter viewed the world differently, expressed themselves differently towards life. It requires no special historical or literary knowledge to discern the countenance of the new woman from the mass of women of the past. We cannot always give an account of what this *novum* consists of, or pinpoint wherein the difference actually lies. One thing, however, is clear: somewhere in the realm of the subconscious a criterion has been formed in us with the aid of which we can classify and determine the feminine types.

Who, then, are these new women? They are not the pure, "nice" girls whose romance culminates in a highly successful marriage, they are not wives who suffer from the infidelities of their husbands, or who themselves have committed adultery. Nor are they old maids who bemoan the unhappy love of their youth, just as little as they are "priestesses of love," the victims of wretched living conditions or of their own depraved natures. No, it is a wholly new "fifth" type of heroine, hitherto unknown, heroines with independent demands on life, heroines who assert their personality, heroines who protest against the universal servitude of woman in the State, the family, society, who fight for their rights as representatives of their sex. Single women are the ones who more and more determine this type. The "single woman": in the most recent past the original type of woman was the "spouse," the wife who was the shadow of the husband, a supplement, an appendage. The single woman has ceased to play this subordinate role and to be no more than the reflex of the man. She has a singular inner world, full of general human interests, she is independent inwardly and self-reliant outwardly. Twenty years ago, a statement of this kind would have said nothing either to the mind or to the heart. The girl, the mother, the "blue stocking" (not viewed in her problematic aspects), the beloved, or the salon-lioness of the stripe of Elena Kurakina (Tolstoy, *War and Peace*), all these personages exemplified an understandable, traditional staple of fiction. But for the single woman there was no place either in literature or life. If women emerged in history with features that recalled contemporary heroines, they were viewed as random deviations from the norm, as psychological phenomena.

But life does not stand still, the wheel of history, which turns at an ever faster tempo, compels even persons of the one and same generation to form new concepts, to enrich their lexicon with new material. The single woman, of which our grandmothers and even our mothers had no idea whatsoever, exists. She is a real, living phenomenon.

Single women. They are the million figures, wrapped in drab clothing, who pour out of the working-class quarters in an endless train on their way to work sites and factories, who set out for the circular railways and the tramcars in that hour before daybreak in which dawn still battles with the darkness of night. Single women. They are those tens of thousands of young, already fading, women who settle down in the big cities in lonely room-cages and increase the statistic of "independent" households. They are girls and women who ceaselessly wage the grim struggle for existence, who spend their days sitting on the office chair, who bang away at telegraph apparatuses, who stand behind counters. Single women: they are the girls with fresh hearts and minds, full of bold fantasies and plans who pack the temples of science and art, who crowd the sidewalks, searching with vigorous and virile steps for cheap lessons and casual clerical jobs. We see single women seated at a worktable preparing a laboratory experiment, burrowing through archival material, rushing off to hospital patients, drafting a political speech.

How dissimilar are these images to the heroines of the recent past! To the bewitching, touching women of Turgenev, Chekhov, to the heroines of Zola, Maupassant, the impersonal, good-hearted feminine types of German and English literature, even of the '80's and of the beginning of the '90's. Life creates the new women—literature reflects them.

A succession of heroines of the new type pass in review before us in an endless motley train. The woman writer Mathilde[1] pushes her way forward through the thick, prickly thorny undergrowth of the present reality, clearing a path with a calm, proud,

1. From Karl Hauptmann's novel *Mathilde*.

determined gait. The thorns of life tear at her hands and feet till the blood flows, lacerate her breast. But there is no wincing in this face, becoming stonelike and as hard as steel as a result of life's cares and torments, even though the bitter lines around the mouth dig deeper, even though the glance, proud and unbowed, beams with bold brilliance.

A new suffering: a beam of joy—a guest who alights rarely on working-class circles—darts by without affecting her. Mathilde stands on the mountain, proud, unshakeable, wrapped in her gray shawl. A statue of sadness. But her gaze is fixed upon the unknown—she sees "the future," she believes in it. Mathilde, steeled by earlier skirmishes with life, comes to the city. Freshness, youth, health ooze from her. So she knocked on the factory gate and entered the work site. The brick monster has swallowed another victim. But Mathilde is not afraid of life. Confident and proud, she steps over the snares that fate mockingly sets for her, the lonely, meditative girl, the dirt and vulgarities of life do not besmirch her. Mathilde bears her clear, pure human "ego" though life with an unshakable naïveté. She is only a lonely, poor factory girl, but she is proud of what she is, she is proud of her inner strength, proud of the fact that she is absolutely self-reliant. Then the first inclination—tender and radiant as youth itself—the first joys of motherhood. The first sensation of loving dependency, a timid rebellion against the loss of freedom. Then again, the wave of a new, torrid passion. The pangs, torments of love, longing, hurt, disappointment and then again loneliness. But we are not in the presence of a bowed "lost" girl, of a pathetic, depressed creature—no, before us stands a proud, lonely mother—a human being turning in upon herself. Mathilde's personality grows and strengthens itself, and every new suffering, every new page of life merely shows her strong, unshakeable "ego" in bolder relief.

Compared to her the dreamy Tatiana, the girl from Riasan,[2] treads softly in bare feet, burnt and chapped by sun and storm. She goes around with people as homeless and as shelterless as herself. "A piece of copper on a rubbish heap of old rust-eaten iron." Today she busies herself in Maikopa at the time of the hay harvest, and tomorrow she wanders to the Don with a troop of agreeable comrades. These people go whither they scent the possibility of earning wages.

Tatiana goes along with them. Free as the wind, lonely as the grass on the steppes. She is dear to nobody. No one will protect her. Eye to eye, breast to breast, she wages an unbroken, tireless struggle against fate. And pitiless fate ruffles her, it shows her no tenderness, it has only hardness for single women like Tatiana and Mathilde. But Tatiana does not bow under the blows of life's scourge, for a long time she does not bow and deeply hidden in her soul she bears her earthly dream, the dream that is shown to her by a clear, unruffled summer night—the future. Thus she goes through the world and seeks her happiness. But, as if to mock her, happiness only draws farther and farther away from Tatiana. The dreamy-tender girl from Riasan gleans only the crumbs of a fugitive happiness.

A passerby stirs her soul, she weeps, is inflamed and gives herself to him. Simply and straightforwardly she wrests for life her small earthly joys to which such single women—and understandably so—migrant women workers precisely give themselves. But she does not want to bind her life to the passerby: "That's not for me—no, I don't like that! Yes, if only you were a peasant!

2. From Maxim Gorki's *Notes of a Passerby*.

But this way, it makes no sense! That might do for an hour, but not for a whole life!"

And she goes forth, gently smiling at him in farewell, she goes forth in search of the happiness of which she dreams, she goes forth lost in her own thoughts, as though she were alone in the world, and as though everything willed to be created anew by her.

Thus Mathilde and Tatiana go thither, they break through the undergrowth of life and with their breasts and hands they clear the path to the longed-for future. But, behind them, the new women of other social strata press forward, full of zeal to reach the newly laid-out path. They, too, are torn and wounded by the branches of the prickly thorn bushes; their feet, unused to walking on sharp stones, are also sore, and their footsteps are also left behind in red streaks of blood. But there is no such thing as standing still: thick, impenetrable undergrowth over and over again closes off the new path, but the path nevertheless widens more and more. Woe to those who succumb to weakness! Woe to the enfeebled! Woe to those who look backward into the ever vanishing past! They will be pushed off the path by the serried ranks of those who are pressing forward.

And, with bowed heads, the weary sink down on the edge of the new path and look back on the gray castle of their former slavery.

In the serried ranks of those who seek a new path, we look for, we discern heroic women—physiognomies of all nations, of all social strata. In front of them all gleam the beauteous features of the actress Magda,[3] this artist so proud of her maidenly and

3. Sudermann, *Heimat.*

human dignity with the bold motto of the new woman: "I am I—and what I am, I became on my own ability." Magda has broken with the traditions of a provincial bourgeois family and has challenged bourgeois morality to its face. But, proud, the "sinner" remains under her parents' roof, in the "homeland." Magda knows the worth of her personality and staunchly defends her right to be herself. To rise above her sins is more to her than the pharisaical purity in which the bourgeois world lives.

The bold, clever, passionate Olga[4] sets out determinedly on the new path. She breaks away from a patriarchial Jewish family, overcomes one obstacle after another, and plunges into the hurly-burly of life in a big European city. She is accepted in an elect circle of intellectuals, "the cream of society," and the life of this center of culture and capitalism gaily unfolds before her. The struggle for existence, the struggle against the unemployment plaguing intellectuals, the struggle for self-assertion as human being and as woman! Olga lives, as do thousands of intellectual young women in the big urban cultural centers—alone in the struggle for existence. Olga does not fear life and boldly demands from fate her quota of personal happiness. The man whom Olga loves is at once near and far. Their life-paths cross from time to time. Building a common life together does not correspond to the interests of either. Love merely grazes her rich store of experience. Passion wanes—thereupon love also dies. They go their separate ways. And again we do not behold a young woman, weak, suffering, bowed, but a human being who bravely drains the cup in which the wine is mixed with poison. Olga is stronger than the one chosen by her. In the hours of unhappiness, even

4. Greta Meisel-Hess, *Die Intellektuellen*.

of love's sorrow, he hastens to Olga as to his only, sincere friend. In the tangled, rich experiences and struggle for existence, love's romance, for Olga, is only an introductory "episode."

In the multitude of the new women, the woman doctor Laucorojelo,[5] the typical single woman, strides with sure step, her beautiful head held high. Science and the practice of medicine constitute the substance of her life. The clinical wards are at once her temple and her home. She fights for recognition and respect among her male colleagues; gently but unyieldingly she rejects all attempts to win her over to marriage. She needs to be free and alone for her beloved activity, without which she cannot live. She is severe in dress, she apportions her time strictly, she struggles to acquire a practice and experiences the triumph of self-love with the victory over her male colleagues as diagnostician. The image of the "emancipated woman" as cold already begins to come across to the reader. Then, as if by accident, we glimpse another scene and, for the first time, we see the woman doctor from a wholly different aspect. It's the holiday season and with her "friend"—likewise a doctor—she is seeking recreation in the country. Here she is woman—here the femine "ego" gets the upper hand. Her clothes are now light and colorful, her smile gladsome. She makes no secret of her "bond," and when she does not live together with the friend in Paris, this happens only because it is more "convenient" to both of them—the colleagues—this way.

The passionate Theresa,[6] all fire, all zeal, rushes by the great woman doctor! She is an Austrian socialist, a fiery agitator. She has served time in prison. She plunges into Party work with her

5. Collette Ivere, *Princesses of Science.*
6. Schnitzler, *Der Weg ins Freie.*

whole heart and soul. But when she, too, is overwhelmed by the waves of passion, she does not deny the radiant smile of life, she does not hide hypocritically behind the faded mantle of womanly virtue—no, she reaches out her hands to the chosen one, she remains for several weeks away from the scene of her activity, in order to drink the joys of love from the goblet and to convince herself how deep it is. And when she drains it to the dregs, she casts it away without regret, without bitterness. And she goes back to her work. For Theresa, as for the majority of her male comrades, love is only a stage, only a brief respite on life's path. The aim of her life, its content, is the Party, the idea, agitation and propaganda work.

Another of the new women, Agnes Petrovna,[7] one of the first Russian heroines of the type of the single woman, chooses her path with calm circumspection. She is a writer, an editorial secretary, but she is "above all a working human being." When Agnes is working, when any thought, any idea, takes hold of her, nothing else and nobody exists for her. "I cannot separate myself from it, and for this I need freedom and I will not sacrifice my freedom for any kind of love whatsoever." But when Agnes comes home and changes her working clothes for a comfortable house dress, then it gives her joy to acknowledge herself unreservedly as woman and to try her feminine charm on men. She seeks neither the substance nor the goal of life in love, but only that which most men also seek for in it: "Diversion, poetry, light." But she herself does not recognize any power over herself, over her "ego," on the part of the beloved man.

"To belong to a man like an object, to give him one's whole will, one's whole heart, one's whole understanding, and to gear

7. T. Stschepkina-Küpernik, *One of Them.*

61

the employment of all one's energies exclusively to his well-being —and to do this with full consciousness and joyfully—all that can probably make a woman happy. But why all this for only one person? ... If one must forget oneself, then I would rather do it not just for one person alone, by preparing a good noon meal and a restful slumber for him; if such be the case I will grant all that also to such-and-such other unhappy ones . . ."

And when Miatlev attempts to interfere with her freedom, when he dares to place his love between her and her work, her writing activity, Agnes considers the bond dissolved and they come to a parting of the ways.

Slowly with a tinge of insecurity, Agnes is followed by a less sharply sketched portrait of another single woman: Vera Niko-dimovna.[8] Vera has been raised in the traditions of the old generation with a touch of modernism. She has "a past," and this past, which ended in "an awful, awful, banal way," has left a dark mark on her soul. It is not only the "physiological" that drives the reflective and almost frigid Vera into men's embraces. "Nobody knows how little one's feeling is involved in this, how little it all has to do with wantonness," she confesses to her young lady friend. Something different stands behind it. What was it exactly? The longing for motherhood! Perhaps the search for a kindred, understanding soul, this dangerous angel remains fastened to the soberly reflective single women. Ever since her confession Vera is surrounded by men who adore her. But—instincts inherited from grandmothers ward off the approaches of men whom she lures with hopes. Being a temptress becomes her specialty. But in contrast to the grandmothers, unmoved, she holds onto her freedom and, besides being a drawing-room flirt,

8. Potapenko, *In the Fog.*

Vera Nikodimova is a working, thinking woman-human being.

The sadly smiling image of consumptive Mery[9] floats by. Behind her comes the diminutive, courageous fighter Talia,[10] who looks for work in her clattering, worn-out shoes. Behind them rings the repulsive laughter of the intellectually impoverished, shallow Annette,[11] who in this novel and in her way is a parody of the single woman. Robust-naïve Anna, Sanschar's heroine,[12] presses forward along the new path. Mira, Lydia, and Nelly[13] stride forth, arm in arm. Each one has something quite special, holy, not only womanliness. We find this vanity, this ambition, even with the seemingly vapid Lydia. But as soon as love is kindled, as soon as the feminine nature demands its rights, all these young women cross the forbidden threshold without the former sentimental fear of themselves. But later the polytonal symphony of life, in which love is only an introductory melody, again tears them away.

The music hall *artiste* glides by, dodging the sharp stones, with her finesse of soul that enchants our eyes, as though she was formed out of soft aquarelle tones. She has left her husband with her illusions shattered, a wounded heart; she has thrown down the gauntlet to the world to which she belonged. Her life now belongs to art, which she practices in mime dances and pantomime that she herself composes. It is a nomadic, wearying, strenuous life. She seeks no adventure—she wards them off: her heart has been too deeply wounded. Freedom, independence, solitude are the substance of her personal desires. But when René, after

9. Winnitschenko, *On Life's Scale*.
10. *Ibid*.
11. *Ibid*.
12. Sanschar, *Anna's Notes*.
13. Collette Villi, *La Vagabonde*.

a tiring long day's work, sits at the fireplace in her lovely flat, it is as though the hollow-eyed melancholy of loneliness creeps into her room and sets himself behind her chair.

"I am used to being alone," she writes in her diary, "but today I feel so forsaken. Am I then not independent, not free? And terribly lonely?" Does not this question have the ring of the woman of the past who is used to hearing familiar, beloved voices, to being the object of indispensable words and acts of tenderness?

And when passion suddenly invades René on her paths, she allows herself to succumb to the advancing waves and to be borne away by them. But passion does not blind her, it does not becloud her analytical mind.

"Only my senses are attacked," she establishes with melancholy regret. "Only my senses are intoxicated." René sobers up. The new love does not give her what she had been seeking. In the embrace of the beloved she is as lonesome as before. And "la Vagabonde" flees, she fades from her love, she flees because this love is so unlike the refined demands she makes on love.

René's farewell letter to her abandoned friend is a document of the contemporary woman touching on the soul's new claims and demands on life. Benette's[14] heroine steps forth behind her. She is a writer, a single woman. Ecstasy and adoration drive her into the arms of a great musician, but the experience only helps her to find and strengthen her own identity, to prove her writing talent, and to take a more sober, more reflective, and more conscious stance towards life. And when, later, a new love approaches, she does not flee from it, like the heroines of earlier English novels who, beshamed, viewed themselves as dishonored,

14. Benette, *Holy Love.*

fallen creatures. Rather, she goes towards the new love, smiling.

The restless, temperamental Maya[15] impetuously pushes forward. She has an ironical disposition. To her, all experiences are but stages on the way to herself—to the shaping of her personality: struggle with her relatives for independence, separation from the first husband, a brief romance with an Oriental hero, a second marriage, full of refined psychological details. Thereupon, a bitter struggle is waged in Maya's soul between the old and the new femininity; there is another separation, again a new seeking until Maya finally finds the man who exhibits respect for her inner "voice," this symbol of personality, who recognizes her importance and knows how to create an inwardly free love bond about which Maya has dreamt all her life.

Maya's life harbors a profusion of psychological complications and experiences. But all that from which a woman of the old stamp would have broken long ago (the infidelity of the beloved man, the break with two men) serves Maya only as education, allows her to arrive at self-understanding all the more surely. Unconsciously, she follows Goethe's counsel: "to begin one's life anew every day, as though it were just beginning . . ." "My stronger, more courageous will, which nothing could break, saved me—my unconscious will to self-preservation. It led me through life like a guardian angel," says Maya of herself.

Nevertheless there are still enough episodes in Maya's life that recall the old breed. The new, independent, inwardly free woman constantly struggles with the atavistic inclination to be the "shadow of the husband," his echo. How familiar in her is the naïve conscientious effort to arrange herself inwardly so as to accord with the taste of her husband whom she loves, to perfect

15. Grete Meisel-Hess, *The Voice*.

herself fully in keeping with the ideal that her chosen one had formed of her. As though she had no worth of her own, as though her personality was to be appraised only according to the relation men had towards her. This atavistic trait in women is so strong that even so splendid, brilliant, bewitching a personality as George Sand could be tempted to wish to forsake the world for the sake of a rapturous Musset and then, later, to renounce the flight to the stellar world of artistic creation for the sake of sober politics. But the strong personality of George Sand drew a line against such experiments. The moment came when George Sand sensed that she was about to lose her identity, that by such adjustment the woman in her—Aurore Dudevant—was directing George Sand, the bold, rebellious, passionate dreamer, to destruction and stifling her.

Then George Sand tore the former bonds with no regrets. And when once such a decision was born in her soul, nothing could hold her back, no power, not even her own passion was able to break the will of this great human being with the bewitching, tender-receptive, feminine soul.

When Aurore Dudevant leaves her estate on a gloomy autumn day for a last brief farewell with her lover, even though the decision to break with him is already ripened and formalized— we need have no concern over George Sand—we feel that this encounter cannot have the force to change her decision, it is nothing else but the last gift of a dissolving passion which George Sand flings to the weeping Aurore. The stage is surpassed, the experience is closed, and that is all.

Meisel-Hess's Maya, naturally, is not of the same stature of George Sand, she is much weaker. But in her, too, a limit is set to her adaptation to the beloved. Her atavistic inclination to self-denial, to self-alienation and dissolution in love, collides with her already developed, distinct human personality. Maya also understands how to straighten herself out in a given moment and she goes forth in order to save her "voice."

How difficult it is for today's woman to cast aside this capacity, internalized in the course of centuries, of millenniums, with which she tried to assimilate herself to the man whom fate seemed to have singled out to be her lord and master. How difficult she will find it to convince herself that woman must reckon self-renunciation as a sin, even a renunciation for the sake of the beloved and for the sake of the power of love.

The cold, reflective, ambitious Uta[16] steps impressively alongside Maya. Uta is an actress, her whole life is a continuous display and adornment of her own "ego" which to her stands far higher than anything else in the world. It is as though art, too, is dear to her only as a further means for the unfoldment and revelation of her strong personality, only more fully and in a many-faceted way. It shows the natural reaction against the centuries—long self-abasement of woman and her submissive renunciation of the right to be a personality with a characteristic value of her own. Strong, passionate ambition, cold reasoning, extraordinary selfishness and a striking talent for the stage get the upper hand in her and drive Uta into a dark corner. Calmly, she passes up personal happiness, Klodt's boundless devotion. She appreciates his love, because she loves to glimpse her splendor reflected therein, as in a mirror. When Klodt, confused by Uta's glamor, tormented by her cold indifference, betrays her before her eyes, she weeps. But it is not the woman in her that is offended. Rather it is the artist who is exposed to all admiring gazes, whose particular wor-

16. Heinrich Mann, *On the Hunt for Love.*

67

shipper has dared to go over to her rival, to the hated Fronchini. It is not outraged love that weeps in her, but wounded egotism. Uta remains true to herself up to the end of the novel—she carries her spiritual coldness and her adoration of her own "ego" through life. But, in Uta, is it not the absence of that "holy flame" which makes "great" artists, which makes the frivolous, temperamental "wifie" Fronchini carry off the victory over the clever, cultivated Uta, who is much more developed and even "important," in her art, but devoid of temperament?

The artist Tania,[17] spoiled by life, shines forth in the multitude. Although Tania is a married woman, one cannot but include her in the type of "single woman," as with Maya, even though she was formally married three times. It is in keeping with her inner physiognomy. For instance, does not Tania, although she lives together with her lawful spouse under the same roof, remain free and independent as before and as a human being, "herself"? She frowns when her husband introduces her to his friends without mentioning her own name. Each of them lives in a world of his own, she in the world of art, he in the world of his professorship, of science. They are good friends, comrades, strong bonds unite them, but as good friends they do not curtail one another's freedom.

Tania's blind, physiological passion for the handsome "manikin" Stark invades this pure atmosphere. In Stark, naturally, Tania does not love the intellectual physiognomy, not his soul, but the "eternal masculine" with which he drew her like a magnet at their first meeting. She flits by his soul, just as up to now men have flitted by the souls even of passionately loved women, stretching their arms in defensive helplessness when the "adored"

17. Nagrodskaya, *The Anger of Dionysius.*

Anna, Manya, or Lisa, amid tears, utter the familiar reproach: "But your soul, your soul, that you don't give . . ." Tania's attitude towards Stark altogether bears the stamp of the male. We feel that she, as a personality, is both clearer and stronger, as well as richer than he. Tania is too much a human being, too little "wifie" for naked passion to be able to satisfy her. She herself admits that her passion for Stark does not enrich her soul, but impoverishes it, dries it out. It is characteristic that Tania suffers less from the consciousness of her infidelity to her husband than from the tormenting realization that comes to her in moments when she yields to amorous rapture, of the irreconcilability of such love with planful, enduring work without which she cannot live.

Passion consumes her energies, her time and makes free, creative work impossible. Thus, Tania begins to lose herself and that which to her is the dearest thing in life. Tania goes back to her husband but not because "duty" enjoins it, and even less out of pity, but out of love for herself, in order to save her identity and her personality.[18]

She can lose herself with Stark. She goes back and is with child by Stark. She goes back, but not because the passion is already extinct. Where is the heroine of the novels of the good old times who would have possessed so much bravery as to act like Tania?

Tania faces the choice which in her time was faced by one of the first heroines of the psychologically new type of woman—

18. Here the author should have written *finis* to his novel. The whole further romance with Stark is contrived. In the Tania accommodating herself to circumstances, renouncing her art, who has become nothing else but an object of pleasure for Stark, we no longer recognize the earlier, bold, coherent personality of Tania the human being. It is regrettable that the author so slanders his Tania.

Ibsen's Ellida. Since the "man from the sea" demands that she follow him, and her husband accords her full freedom of choice —Ellida remains with her husband. She remains in the consciousness that, thereby, she is saving her inner freedom, whereas she would forfeit it if she were to go off with the "man from the sea." Ellida has understood that she was threatened by the most terrible captivity imaginable for a woman—the captivity of passion, a power that he held over her feminine heart.

The psychically stoic, the spiritually strong Josepha[19] modestly clears her path and proffers a helping hand to those on the edges of the path beset by the still protruding, prickly branches of the thorny bushes of life. She helps the women of bourgeois society beat a path to economic independence, she shows them the way to the professions. The sensitive, cautious Christa Ruland[20] gropes hesitantly along the path. We have here a bewitching, tender portrayal of a grown woman who with big, wide-opened eyes peers questioningly into the world in which she seeks the new rights for woman, and, at the same time, first begins to become conscious of herself. Her motto is: "I—and I and you— are you, we are one only in love."

The heroine of Juschkevitsch's novel, Elena,[21] hiding the tragedy of her soul, the tormenting, strange world-weariness which is not comprehensible even to her, presses forward on the margin of the path to the "new rights." She is not single and not even one of the "new women" in the actual sense of the word. In her psyche, the traits of the new and the old type have entangled and formed a complicated knot. The eternal feminine

19. Ilse Frapan, *Work*.
20. Hedwig Dohn, *Christa Ruland*.
21. Juschkevitsch, *Secession From the Circle*.

is clear and strong in her, but her mind, her human "ego," fills the tender feminine soul with grave questions. She is sacrificing, affectionate, full of feminine contradictions and even of slavish mendacities, but her rebellious, endlessly seeking, questioning mind makes out of Elena a figure of a new kind. Juschkevitsch has presented her in soft tones and treated the character so circumspectly, so affectionately as though fearful of breaking with a word this sensitive, fragile feminine soul whose tragic situation finally destroys her.

We distinguish Renate Fuchs[22] in the multitude of the new women, this "rebellious soul" who succeeds in preserving her spiritual purity while she goes through shame, dishonor, and dirt. A lofty calm is spread over her countenance and in her virginal hands she holds the little child, the "new man" of the future. Alongside her steps Greni Allena's heroine[23] proudly guiding by the hand her little daughter, the child of her love from a union which demonstratively had avoided the legal form. The chemist Maria[24] sets foot into her laboratory with officious gestures—her smile is radiant; she has found life's harmony. The prostituted Mylada[25] with head held high bears her "holy mission" through the filth of life which has robbed her of her eyesight.

The social-revolutionary Anna Siemenovna,[26] while concealing herself behind the mask of the coquettish "wifie," deliberately strides through her own passion beginning to end. Leaving the world's prejudices far behind, the emancipated student English-

22. Jacob Wasserman, *Renate Fuchs.*
23. Greni Allena, *The Woman Who Dared.*
24. Winnitschenko, *On the Path of Life.*
25. Else Jerusalem, *The Holy Scarabus.*
26. O. Runow, *Struggle.*

71

woman Fanny[27] glides along with soaring steps and carries her
fragrant clothes unhurried through life's thorny underbrush. Another familiar face beams at us, that of the woman student from
the far north—Anna Mahr[28] . . . Thus do the different heroines
of Björnson, Jonas Lie (*The Commandant's Daughters*), Jakob-
sen, Löffler torment themselves on the new path. Jenny,[29] the
heroine of the Norwegian woman novelist Undset, enters upon
the new path full of restlessness, and always as though she was
harking to voices in her soul reminiscent of the woman of the
past. Like Nagrodskaya's Tania, she leaves the father of her still
unborn child so that motherhood may not strengthen the love
that has begun to be burdensome to her. Now she presses forward
on the new path, with increasing boldness, but a voice of the past
lives in her, reawakens forgotten feelings, conceptions, and ideas.
Jenny pauses in her forward march and looks back—and thereupon she falls to pieces . . .

But ever new figures of awakening, "rebellious," seeking
women press forward beyond her.

The tender, bewitching silhouette of Françoise Houdon,[30] with
her comradely love for Christophe and her passion for another,
with her flaming temperament, full of insatiable artistic ambition,
with an iron will and a fragile, tender soul. On the same line
with her steps the unvarnished, living type of the working woman
Cecile,[31] holdling her soul in balance unconscious of the fact that
the new truth stamps itself in her calm "arrival." The suffragette

27. Bernard Shaw, *Early Debut.*
28. Gerhardt Haupmann, *Lonely People.*
29. Sigrid Undset, *Jenny.*
30. Romain Rolland, *Jean Christophe.*
31. *Ibid.*

Julia France,[32] Marie Antin,[33] the refugee from Russia, the Jewish girl who clears herself a path to American citizenship, to a secure position, and all the heroines of Rikarda Huch, Gabriele Reiner, Sarah Grande, Nemfz Word Krandiewskaia, the symptomatic Baborinin of the salon novelist Marcel Prevost.[35]

There are many of them and they cannot all be listed in this brief sketch. But precisely the fact that there is such a profusion of these new women, who daily appear on the scene in ever new and larger numbers so that their tainted likeness is found even in the boulevard-literature of a Verbitzkaia, proves that life creates and shapes these new types of women without let-up.

This new woman brings with her something alien, that at times repels us because of its newness as a breed, so to speak. We peer at it closely, looking for the familiar, agreeable traits of which our mothers and grandmothers were the bearers. But the

32. G. Aterton, *Julia France and Her Epoch.*
33. Marie Antin, *The Promised Land.*
34. For example, *Rosa, from Vita Somnium Breve.*
35. Most of the authors mentioned are women. Many of their works possess no special artistic worth. Although in and for themselves they are not very talented works, nevertheless they give more with respect to the aim which they have set for themselves than do the artistically superior works of male authors. Most of the novels and short stories that have been written by women are autobiographical, which has the greatest interest for us. The more inartistic and unadorned the full life truth is given, the more fully and more truthfully is the psychology of the new woman presented, its pain, its seeking, its longing, its complications, the richer is the material for the study of the new woman. Since women writers no longer blindly follow male models, since they are now bravely baring the secrets of the feminine soul, which up to now were hidden even from artistic insight, and since women writers have begun to speak their own idiom—a wholly feminine idiom—their works, even though at times lacking in artistic beauty, will assume a special value and significance. They help us, finally, to recognize "the woman," the woman of the type newly being formed.

type who stands before us has broken with the past and harbors within herself a whole world of new feelings, experiences, and demands. Doubt rises in us, we are almost disappointed. Where is the engaging feminine submissiveness and softness of yore? Where is the customary ability of the woman to adjust herself in marriage, to give herself, even vis-à-vis the insignificant husband and to accord him primacy in life?

Before us stands woman as personality, before us stands a human being possessing a characteristic value, with her own individuality, who asserts herself—in short, the woman who has broken the rusted fetters of her sex.

Part Two

WHAT actually are these characterological peculiarities, these new feelings and traits in the feminine psyche that allow us to assign a woman to the class of "single women," according to her inner physiognomy?

Dominance of feeling was the most typical trait peculiar to the woman of the past, and this predominance of feeling at once signified woman's ornament and defect. The sharpening of the economic contradictions in the present, which has drawn woman into the active struggle for existence, makes it imperative that she conquer her feelings, requires that she not only learn to take the protean, social obstacles, but that she also strengthen, through the exercise of her will, her eminently passive, easily yielding spirit, inclined to slackness.

Women have to accomplish a much greater educational mission than men in order for them to be granted the newly fought for rights from life. Gloomy thoughts, grievous cares oppress Josefa in Ilse Frapan's novel, *Work*. Her frail shoulders can hardly bear life's heavy burden. She would like, just once, to be allowed to have herself a good cry, to air all her grievances before someone, as women did formerly; she would like to surrender to her suffering. But the work assigned to her in the clinic according to a strictly laid-out schedule will not wait. She dares not let herself be put off or obstructed from this task by housework or by mending the children's clothes. Josefa must so control herself that her personal life remains hidden as if behind a rail and she arrives at the clinic unfailingly at the stroke of the bell.

Mathilde sees her child die, her joy, everything that was left to her from rapturous love. But her trained fingers work and do not tear the threads of life despite its misery.

Present-day conditions demand from every woman who exercises a trade, a profession, a work of any kind outside the home, so much self-discipline, so much will power, in order to combat her feelings, as was to be found only as an exception to the rule with the woman of the past.

Jealousy, mistrust, the senseless "female revenge," are not these the typical peculiarities of the woman of the past? Jealousy, which lay at the bottom of practically all the tragedies of the feminine soul! Obviously, jealousy also emerged as a tragedy of the male soul. But for his Othello, Shakespeare does not choose a disciplined, civilized Englishman, or an intelligent, refined Venetian, but a Moor ruled by passions.

Women's strong dependency on feeling has misled them to expressing their hatred of rivals in the most hideous forms, and has led them to the borders of woman's busiest, most slavish characteristics. If the heroine has not always exactly poured sulphuric acid over her rival, most probably she overwhelmed her with the poison of her slander.

The new women do not want exclusive possession when they love. Since they demand respect for the freedom of their own feelings, they also learn to accord this respect to others. Characteristic of this is the attitude of the heroine towards the rival as portrayed in a string of contemporary novels. We come upon a tactful, circumspect attitude towards the other woman rather than sulphuric acid and defamatory attacks. Maya and the first wife of her chosen one, in the *Voice,* not only are free from any mutual hatred, but even find a common language and in many things they show more of a closer bond between themselves than with the man to whom the hearts of both belong.

Maya weeps over the offenses that he inflicts on the soul of her rival, when this common "he" treats her as legal property, as an object belonging to him without the heart-warming tendernesses, without the traditional kisses. Maya is offended for "the woman." Maya is able to feel beyond a narrow individualism; in Maya we already have a preview of the feeling of collectivity, of comradeship in love, utterly alien to the old type.

Is not the attitude of the same Maya towards the unnecessary, senseless infidelity of her second husband also characteristic? She catches him red-handed, but Maya doesn't swoon or create a scandal. She leaves the scene forthwith and hastens to the tiny bed of her husband's children by his first wife. These sleeping tots scare away the sadness from her soul. She goes back to her home, grown lonely.

It feels chilly. Maya starts a fire, wraps herself in her shawl and forces herself to read an interesting book. Thus does she swiftly escape herself, thus does she find the necessary balance.

Irina, in the novel by Kredo (*In the Fog of Life*), not only achieves a reconciliation with Victor's former lady friend, but demands a solicitous attitude towards the sensibility of her rival. In return, Victor, when he learns about Irina's past, asks in the tone of the offended "little man": "What number am I on your list? I want to know . . . Were they many?" Victor is a progressive-minded person, a writer, but in him, too, the "animal" is stronger than in the nonentity Irina whose personality is interesting only to the extent that she, too, reaches out for the new truth of life.

In the new woman, the human being increasingly conquers the jealous "wifie."

The far higher demands made on the man, to which Ellen Kay also refers in her writings, are to be viewed as a second typical trait of the contemporary woman. The woman of the past had been raised by her lord and master to adopt a negligent attitude towards herself, to accept a petty, wretched existence as a natural fate. But she puts up with men's condescending smile over her feminine frailities and afflictions without demanding attention for that which she thinks, for that which she experiences. Do not men still express astonishment when their attention is drawn to the fact that hardly one of them ever lent an ear to his wife, even during the minutes of the most intimate experiences? This boundless, inconsiderate attitude to the feminine "ego" was also the cause of family tragedies, formerly.

The experienced Don Juans not only understood how to take a woman's body, but they also ruled her soul, in that most of them acted out the comedy "of understanding," exhibiting a tender-solicitous attention to their unimportant "ego," which her own husband inconsiderately and indifferently passed by. But Don Juans came and went, and the lawful spouse remained and in the course of centuries the woman adjusted herself to this life, reduced her claims and demands, and oriented her conception of happiness on the gratification of the external, of what was objectively tangible.

"He" gave her rings and earrings, "he" brought her flowers and candies, *ergo* he loved her.

But when he became despotic and coarse, when he made demands and laid down prohibitions, this was precisely within his rights, the rights of the master of her heart!

The contemporary woman is demanding, she seeks for and enjoins esteem for her personality, her sensibility. She demands respect for her "ego." She does not endure despotism. When her oriental master forbids Maya to sing at concerts, and when he hears about the transgression of his prohibition and decides "as punishment" not to write to her for two whole weeks, he kills her feeling for him by so doing. He wanted to "punish" her who had, after all, freely given him her heart!

This insistence upon inner freedom recalls an old legend of women of the earliest times. "Thy will has been done, but thou has lost thy wife in me"—Rosamunde hurls these words at her royal consort when he forces her to drink from the skull of her murdered father. And this is no empty threat because she kills the man whom, up to then, she has passionately loved.

The modern woman can forgive much to which the woman of the past would have found very difficult to reconcile herself: the husband's inability to provide for her material maintenance, lack of attention of an external kind, even infidelity, but she never forgets or forgives the non-esteem of her spiritual "ego," of her sensibility.

When the friend has "no ear" for this, for the new woman, her association with him loses half of its worth.

When Christa Ruland's beloved, in answer to her question of what he thinks about women, at first is evasive and then comes out with banal platitudes, Christa involuntarily feels estranged. How could he, who won her soul with his solicitous attitude, prove so deaf to Christa's intellectual "ego" by not instinctively understanding how important it was to hear his opinion of women's intellectual importance? Christa does not forgive him for this, just as no new woman would forgive this infidelity of men which they believe, or fancy, surely to possess. The same woman whom the husband loves for the sake of her bold flight, because of her psychic independence, he seeks to secure for himself by extinguishing the "holy light" in her with the help of which she has sought her path, by trying to reduce her to an object of his pleasure, of his enjoyment. Christa notices with astonishment how the same Frank, who had vigorously tried to draw her into the sphere of his own intellectual interests, who dreamt of political propaganda tours together, begins to detach himself from her and to close himself off from her in his own intellectual world. There is no more talk, naturally, of taking trips together. And even in the minutes in which Christa eagerly follows his intellectual pursuits the only thing to which he responds is to the woman in her and this all the more captivatingly the more cultivated and thoroughly intellectualized she is. It is as though her intellectuality, with her capacity to rise with him to his non-mundane realm of ideas, only sharpens his sexual appetence for her. Christa leaves him as though she were "stealing away."

The new woman forgives an affront to the "wifie" in her, but she never forgets the least inattentiveness vis-à-vis her personality. With Vera Nikodimovna it is a question of the same demands on the intellectual personality of the chosen one. According to Vera the mind, even an "excellent" one, plays a subordinate role in woman: "The main thing with her is the moral foundation. And, in fact, when we educate ourselves and read, this moral foundation remains stationary almost without development. And how unhappy we are, then! Men then, in most cases, do not understand what there is about them that displeases and repels us . . ."

The demand set forth by women that the man should love and appreciate not so much the impersonal-feminine, but rather that which presents their spiritual substance, their individual "ego," grew naturally on the basis of self-knowledge as personality. "I curse my female body; because of it you do not notice that there is still something else in me—something more valuable"—that is the cry that is heard through the whole novel of Nadjescha Sanschar (*Anna's Notes*). And heroines of all nationalities repeat this protest in this or that form. Even the simple soul of Gorki's Tatiana protests against an attitude that brands her as a single instrument of pleasure.

"He could have had me . . . But I don't want to, I can't, that way, without heart, like a cat . . . What kind of people are you . . . so coarse . . ."

The sharper the personality of the woman is stamped, the more consciously does she feel herself as a "human being," the more sharply does she understand the offense that lies in the fact that the man, with a psychology blunted in the course of centuries, was not able to see in the desired woman the awakening human being, the personality.

These increased demands on the men are the warrant for the fact that so many heroines of modern novels hurry from one enjoyment to another, from one love to another in the wearying search for their ideal: harmony between passion and spiritual kinship, the reconciliation of love and freedom, comradeship with mutual independence.

"There's nothing I long for so passionately as to find a man from whom I would no longer desire to leave, from whom I

81

would not want to go away," exclaims Maya the restless seeker. And the "Vagabond" leaves her friend only because there dwells within her the inextinguishable ideal of a still greater, still more perfect community of love. Present-day reality disenchants all the ingenuous seekers of a harmonious, total love. They tear the bonds of love without regret and resume the search for their ideal. And thereby they forget that what they want to find now, at best, can exist as a life-possibility only in the distant future among people with a new psychic structure, among people who have organically internalized the idea that comradeship and freedom must occupy first place also in love-relationships.

The woman of the old type had been altogether ignorant of how to appreciate personal independence. What would she have done with it anyway? What can be more pathetic, helpless, than an abandoned wife or beloved when she belongs to the old type? With the departure or death of her husband the wife not only lost her material maintenance, but her one and only moral support collapsed. Unaccustomed to an eyeball-to-eyeball confrontation with life, the woman of the past feared being alone and was ready to free herself at the first opportunity from that independence which she had found so unpleasant and unnecessary.

The contemporary, new woman not only has no fear of independence, but she learns to appreciate it, increasingly, to the degree that her interests go beyond the narrow circle of the family, of the home, and of love. For Vera Nikodimovna there can be nothing more terrible than material dependency on a man: "Oh, how unhappy I would be if I were dependent on a man, and if I had to hunt for one to become my husband and therefore be under the obligation to keep me! Oh, how wretched I would be!" she says to her friend.

To have a "husband," a proprietor of and ruler of her soul—
the thought terrifies Vera no less than the thought of prison must
terrify the prisoner who has finally escaped to freedom. "I would
never give myself to this slavery . . ."

"Are you married?"

"No, I'm not married, but I have had my romance and my
passion."

The woman of the present feels in marriage a fetter, even
when no outer, formal bond exists. The psyche of the old human
being that still lives in us creates fetters of a moral nature incomparably stronger than the outer ones. All the more stubbornly
does the new heroine flee all that which could bind her to the
ruler of her heart even externally. It was material dependency
on men, complete helplessness in life, above all, that drove the
woman of the past to structure her relations to the man in such
a way as to ensure their indissolubility. Only then did she feel
out of danger. The new woman, who is forced independently to
bear life's burden, assumes either a rejecting, or even an indiffer-
ent, attitude towards the form of a firm bond. She is altogether
in no hurry to determine her love-relationships through a form.
In reply to a question as to the nature of René's relationship to
her friend (*La Vagabonde*), whether it has a bourgeois marriage
in view or whether it is a transient love affair, René merely
shrugs her shoulders and blurts out:

"Us? Put simply—we are studying each other."

"And, what about the future?"

"Oh, Margot, I don't like the future!"

Mathilde is in no hurry whatsoever to bind herself to Saljoka,
even though she has a child by him, just as she is in no hurry to
formalize her union with the clerk Dominikus. And, if Erneste

had not gone away, Mathilde, despite her ardent feelings for him, in all probability would have been satisfied with her free union and not fought for her right of formal possession. Reason suggested to her, the aging woman, marriage to him, just as it suggested marriage to him, the aging bachelor. Gorki's Tatiana shows just as little inclination to hasten to bind her fate to that of another. She looks around in the world for a suitable man, according to her ideal. But she does not grant the right of possession even to those upon whom she voluntarily bestows her charms. "It might be all right for an hour, but for life. . . ?"

Every woman who exercises a profession, who serves any cause, an idea, needs independence and personal freedom. Rosa, in *Vita Somnium Breve,* does not interfere with the freedom of her beloved Michael, she leaves him his lawful wife, his family; for years she contents herself with brief, radiant encounters with her friend and beloved. But for the fact that she has elevated to the status of being the substance of her life not her love, but her art, her paintings, does not that "touching renunciation" also live in her? "I'm alone," thinks Rosa, "and nevertheless not alone with my pictures, my thoughts, my creations."

Up to now, the main content of a woman's life was directed upon the experience of love. Love, even for a life overladen with material superfluousness, was still the most beautiful ornament. Conversely, the absence of love made a woman's life colorless, empty, poor. No outer blessing, no honorific distinction could replace the loss of love's happiness in a woman, not even the joys of motherhood![1]

1. It is characteristic that the joy of motherhood was viewed as the surrogate of woman's happiness. If she was not happy with marriage, she also had to renounce a free-love relationship outside the marriage bond;

When the heart was empty, life also seemed empty. It was thus that the women of the past distinguished themselves from the men. With men, their active life still proceeded side by side with their emotional life, and while the heroine pined away with longing for "him," "he," the husband, waged the struggle with fate somewhere in a world which the woman neither grasped nor understood. How many psychological plays are based on the fact that the woman waited, longingly, for "him," for the moment when he would return from his professional absence, from office or work. But, upon his return, instead of occupying himself exclusively with "her" he hurriedly wolfed down his food in order to rush to a meeting, or took his papers out of his briefcase and eagerly plunged into his reading. His wife observed this with absolute incomprehension, her soul seething with reproaches. After all, she could have gladly set aside the blouse she had begun to knit. She could also, for his sake, have left the dishes piled in the kitchen sink, and even put the children to bed early so that, finally, both could be alone, so that for once he could forget the tiresome things: business, work, politics, the office. Women of all social strata suffered from this incomprehension of their husband and his interests which lay in an alien world, far beyond the borders of the domestic nest. This incomprehension of the male psyche was met with all women: with the wife of the professor and the wife of the civil servant alike, of the writer, or of the shop assistant.

if she was widowed, maternal concerns and maternal joys remained as the last refuge. Motherhood was seldom seen as an aim in itself. Only with the aging woman did feelings for the preservation of the species, of the family, awaken and now become her life-goal, her idol which she adored, despotically demanding this adoration also from the other members of the family.

The wife's offended exclamation, "So, already you're off again to your horrible meetings!" often accompanies the husband today, regardless of whether he is a worker or a stock-broker.

But, to the same degree as the woman is being increasingly drawn into the vortex of social life, as she proves herself as an active tiny wheel in the mechanism of the economy, so her own horizon, the walls of her own home, which separated her from the world, collapse, and unconsciously she internalizes its interests which, formerly, were alien and incomprehensible, and she makes them her own. Love ceases to form the only substance of her life; furthermore, it is alloted the subordinate role it plays with most men. To be sure, for the new woman, too, there come periods in her life when love—love, the passion—holds her soul prisoner, when her mind, her heart, and thereby all other interests are eclipsed and thrust into the background. At such times the new woman can experience the crassest dramas, she can enjoy and suffer like the woman of the past. But the state of being in love, passion, love are but transient periods in her life. Its true content is the "holy" that the new woman serves: the social idea, science, creativity. At her work, her ideal is for her, for the new woman, in most cases, more important, more valuable, holier than all the joys of the heart, all the delights of passion.

Her new relation to work, which we do not find among the heroines of the good old days, also stems from this fact. Benette's heroine has just had her first passionate-blissful conversation with the man she loves. But when he tells her he wants to call on her next morning, very early, the beloved, the blissful woman, notwithstanding, interrupts him almost horrifiedly, "But please not before breakfast!"

" 'Not before breakfast'? Why?"

"He was astonished. But in the course of these five years I had grown accusomed to being my own master. My taste, my habits had crystallized, I had created my own arrangement for my life. I never receive anybody before breakfast and I have so much work staring me in the face precisely in the morning. Should I really favor this man as a conqueror, and ruin my morning? A dull anxiety for my freedom, my independence, burgeoned in me." Are these not wholly new traits in the woman in love? A woman who voluntarily dismisses the longed-for encounter with the beloved with its promise of joy, only because she is used to doing her writing in the morning, only because she is pained at the thought of these lost hours taken from work. Could the hours of love, that are devoted to the beloved, ever be considered lost for the woman of the old type?

Tania, in Nagodskaia's novel, torments herself during her honeymoon with Stark in the consciousness of her holiday. Self-reproachfully, she looks at the canvas with the unfinished painting.

"I have promised today to myself and I will ask Stark not to come," she resolves. But Stark (in earlier novels this role would fall to the heroine) is irritated by this and protests.

"A whole day without you," he says in a childish-peevish tone. "I won't disturb you in the least, I'll sit quietly. I'm beginning to become jealous of your art," he says further, "it's too formidable a rival." For this once Tania gives in, but the consciousness that she must neglect her work, keep her model waiting, and be unable to go to the professor, gnaws at her. There is no completeness, no peace in her lovemaking when her love must suffer for its sake.

"Today I am working," she writes triumphantly in her diary, "I work greedily! —I work with joy and have been unable to tear myself away from it since early morning." The diary entry of the balance of the day occurs in bright, high-spirited tones. We feel how a human being has broken the spell of gloom-engendering passions and again found herself. At work, with the palette in hand! Tania is awakened from her dream and suddenly sees that, beyond her and Stark, beyond her narrow atmosphere, generative only of the ecstasies of passion, there exists a great, variegated world, full of joys, beauty, and suffering. Suddenly she remembers her friend Weber, recognizing his utter loneliness. Such are the feelings of a human being who returns home after long absence. Do you find a woman of the old type who would have breathed such a sigh of relief, with almost a tinge of maleness, when upon leaving behind the haze of passion she returns to her neglected work in order, anew, to feel the worth of her own being, as a personality?

Agnes Petrovna (*One of Them*) travels through Italy with her beloved Miatlev, and is rocked to sleep by the gentle lapping of the waves of the Venetian lagoons. Stars, night, gondola ride, love—and suddenly Agnes asks a surprise question: "Can you live this way for long?"

"For an eternity!" he answers. She shudders. Before her lay a life full of kisses, whispering waves, and starry harmony—and it terrifies her.

"Why live then? I'm a woman like all the others," Agnes meditates further, "I'm young and even beautiful, why can't I adjust myself to the idea that for a woman love is everything? But just the thought of an eternity of giving myself to such a pastime drives me out of my mind."

And the same Agnes—immediately she returns to St. Petersburg—jealously draws a line between her work, her writing, against the tyranny of love. In the evening they are a twosome. Then Agnes is suddenly lively, high spirited, "her eyes beamed as she embraced him with a wholly special tenderness and cuddled up to him with a childlike affection, like a kitten . . ." Naturally, Miatlev was about to melt with expectations. But then Agnes bends to his ear and whispers the wholly unexpected confession:

"Beloved, darling! Go home now—I simply must write now, otherwise my thoughts will vanish . . ." The beam in her eyes obviously had nothing to do with him but with the thoughts that suddenly sprouted in Agnes Petrovna's little head . . .

For the woman of the past, the infidelity or the loss of her beloved was the worst possible disaster, in imagination and in fact. But for the heroine of our day what is truly disastrous is the loss of her identity, the renunciation of her own "ego" for the sake of the beloved, for the protection of love's happiness. The new woman not only rejects the outer fetters, she protests "against love's prison itself," she is fearful of the fetters that love, with the stunted psychology peculiar to our time, lays upon lovers. The woman who was habituated to be absolutely consumed in love, even the new woman, assumes an anxious stance towards love. She is constantly fearful that the power of feeling might awaken the slumbering atavistic inclination in her to become the shadow of the husband, might tempt her to surrender her identity, and to abandon her work, her profession, her life-tasks.

This is not a struggle for the "right to love," this is a protest against moral imprisonment, even that of the outwardly freest feeling. This is the rebellion of the women of our age of transition who have not yet learned how to harmonize inner freedom and independence with the all-consuming passion of love.

Whereas the woman of the past, relinquishing love, buried herself in her lightless gray world in order to live in it as a joyless creature, the new woman who has liberated herself from love's servitude, stretches to her full height, proudly and joyfully. "The mental servitude is at an end," rejoices Kredo's heroine after she has convinced herself that the intoxication of passion is past. "No more sorrow, no more excitation, no more fear, she is free, her heart no longer suffers, since Victor whom she has loved has disappeared from her soul, somehow as though unnoticed." And how greatly Irina rejoices because "she feels strength and energy again, which had constantly been depleted in her when she made an effort to draw capital out of the fullness of an alien soul. Such a suppression of her own energies constantly debased her inwardly, and the awakening of these energies therefore brought her joy . . ."

Liberation from the imprisonment of alien thoughts, liberation from pangs and sorrows, these "sharp and mordant offsprings of kisses," to be oneself anew, to find oneself! What a jubilation for a woman who is a personality and what an incomprehensible, utterly unknown feeling for the woman of the past!

A significant transformation had to be effected in the psychic image of woman, her mental life had to develop itself strongly, she had to gather a rich store of intellectual values so that she would not be bankrupt at the moment she ceased to pay her tribute to the man. But precisely for the reason that woman's life is not exhausted in love, for the reason that a great store of ideas and interests is found in her, which make out of her "a human being," we learn to apply a new criterion in the appraisal of woman's moral personality. For centuries, the dignity of the heroine was not measured according to her general human characteristics, not according to her intellectual abilities, nor even according to psychological characteristics, but rather exclusively according to her store of feminine virtues which the property-based bourgeois morality demanded of her. "Sexual purity," sexual virtuousness, were the moral physiognomies of the woman. One who had sinned against the sexual moral code was never forgiven. And the romance writers carefully protected the heroines beloved by them from "falling" and allowed only the non-loved to "sin" as the male heroes sinned, without, of course, having to pay with their moral worth as retribution.

The heroines of contemporary novels in most cases transgress the limits of the usual sexual code of virtues, and regardless of this fact, neither the author nor the reader considers these heroines as "depraved types." We find pleasure in Sudermann's bold Madga, although this young woman has been guilty of a series of "falls." We are touched by the dimension of the humanity of Hauptmann's Mathilde, even though a whole sequence of non-marital associations has passed by us, and even though she has borne children from the different chosen ones of her heart.[2]

Even Vinnitschenko's Dara does not lose her human worth as the result of the unnecessary action of purchased love.

Do not most men act thus and do we not, nevertheless, continue to "respect" them?

A forward movement, imperceptible even to ourselves, has been effected in our psychology in respect to the formation of a new morality. What fifty years ago was considered as a permanent

2. Mathilde's love-adventures do not prevent us from respecting this pure and coherent personality. At the same time, however, we cannot avoid a feeling of pity, mixed with aversion, towards her sister Martha, a worker like herself, who brings money home after her love-adventures. A whole chasm yawns between Mathilde's freedom and Martha's venality.

blot on a woman's or girl's reputation, we now view as a phenomenon requiring neither justification nor forgiveness. In her
time George Sand had to break a lance for the right of a woman
to leave her lawful spouse in order to go to the freely chosen
beloved. In pharisaic England, and not very long ago, Grant
Allan had to take the unwed mother under his wing.

But the old moralistic criterion proves unavailing to the degree
that woman stands on her own feet, that she ceases to be
dependent on the father or on the husband, that she stands side
by side with the husband and participates in the social struggle.

The gradual accumulation of woman's valuable and general
human characteristics teaches us to appreciate in her not the
representative of sex, but the human being, the personality. And
the earlier evaluation of the woman as "wifie," to whom the
husband guaranteed a legal maintenance, withers away by itself.

Life first taught us to apply this standard only to "great
souls": "free" artists, talents, actresses, women writers were
forgiven for their violations of the generally recognized sexual
morality.

"But why should only the 'great souls' set forth this demand?"
rightly asks Bebel. "Why not also the others, who are not great
souls'?

"If Goethe and George Sand—we cite only these two although many have acted similarly—dared to live according to
the promptings of the heart, if Goethe's love-experiences fill
volumes, which are devoured with worshipful rapture by his
readers of both sexes, why condemn others for what in Goethe
and George Sand imbue us with enthusiasm and delight?"[3]

We are pleased to laugh over the hypocrites who refused to

3. A. Bebel, *Woman and Socialism.*

shake the hand of a Sarah Bernhardt because of her immorality, or over the indignant citizens who would have so liked to pull a Magda down from the stage. But when it is a question of "not-great souls," we ourselves often waver and temporarily do not know how we should comport ourselves towards the free, un-married woman! But if, in fact, we were to think of applying to these heroines the moral standard of former centuries, then we must turn away from the most beautiful, most human-feminine personages that modern literature has created. Whereas, at the time when women of the old type, raised in the adoration of irreproachable Madonnas, made an effort to preserve their purity, to make a secret of their feelings and to hide them, it is one of the characteristic traits of the new woman that she does not hide her natural physical drives, which signifies not only an act of self-assertion as a personality, but also as a representa-tive of her sex. The "rebellion" of women against a one-sided, sexual morality is one of the most sharply delineated traits of the new heroine.

This is also natural. In the life of women, the bearers of the future, physiology, in contradiction to the hypocritical views imposed on them, plays an incomparably greater role than with men. Freedom of feeling, freedom in the choice of the beloved, of the possible father of "her" child. The struggle against the fetish of the "double standard"—this is the program that the contemporary heroine tacitly wages in life—from Renate Fuchs up to Hauptmann's Mathilde.

A typical trait of the woman of the past was her renunciation of the power of the flesh, the mask of "immaculateness" which she wore even in marriage. The new woman does not deny her "feminine nature," she does not turn aside from life and does not reject earthly joys which reality smilingly grants to each one coveting them.

Contemporary heroines become mothers without being married, they leave the husband or the beloved, their life can be rich in love-experiences and, notwithstanding, they will count themselves among "fallen creatures" as little as will the author or the modern reader. In the free, frank love-experiences of Mathilde, Olga, or Maya lies an ethic which, perhaps, is more perfect than the passive virtue of a Pushkinian Tatiana or the cowardly morality of a Turgenevian Lisa.

Thus does the new woman present herself to us: self-discipline instead of emotional rapture, the capacity to value her own freedom and independence rather than impersonal submissiveness, the assertion of her own individuality instead of the naïve effort to internalize and reflect the alien image of the "beloved." The display of the right to family happiness instead of the hypocritical mask of virginity, finally the assignation of love-experiences to a subordinate place in life. Before us no longer stands the "wifie," the shadow of the husband—before us stands the personality, the woman as human being.

But who are they, these single new women? How has life created them? The single woman—she is a child of the large-scale capitalist economic system. The single woman is not a rare phenomenon. Rather, as a lawfully repeated, everyday phenomenon she was born simultaneously with the infernal dinning of the machines and the factory sirens calling to work.

Every great transformation still within the sphere of our memory in the conditions of production, and under the impact of the ever newer and newer victories of large-scale capitalist development, compels woman also the adapt herself to the environing reality in the struggle for existence. The woman in the process of formation stands in a relation of closest dependency to the historical stage of economic development which mankind is going through. With the change of economic conditions, with the evolution of the production relations, the inner physiognomy of woman also changes. The new woman could emerge as a type only with the growth in the number of women who were earning their own livelihood.

A half-century ago the participation of woman in industrial life was viewed as a deviation from the norm, as a disturbance of the natural order of things. Even radical minds, even socialists sought for ways of bringing woman back into the home. Today these long outdated and discarded views, at most, are repeated in the prejudices and musty standoffishness of desiccated reactionaries.

A half-century ago, civilized countries counted several tens of thousands, at most one hundred thousand, women in the ranks of the working population. Today the figure of working women already surpasses the male figure. Now civilized nations have available to them not a hundred thousand but millions of women workers. Millions of women, like men, press on the labor market, thousands of women conduct commercial firms, hundreds of thousands have a profession, serve science or art. According to statistics, there are more than sixty million working women in Europe and North America. A more grandiose march of the army of women workers has not yet been seen! And more than 50 per cent of this army are single women, that is to say, such who are totally dependent on their own abilities and who do not follow the old female custom of hanging on the coattails of the "breadwinner."

The production conditions which for many centuries had fettered woman to the home, to the spouse, the breadwinner, unexpectedly have torn away the rusty chains from her and thrust her, the weak, the unprepared sex, onto the newly opened thorny path which draws her into new snares of economic dependency—those woven of capitalism. Under the threat of being shelterless, of suffering hunger and privations, woman learned to stand alone without the support of the father or of the husband. Woman was forced to adjust herself swiftly to the altered conditions of existence. These shattering experiences put to a cruel test the moral axioms on which she had been raised by the grandmothers of the good old days. With astonishment, she was forced to recognize the uselessness of the whole moralistic baggage with which she had been saddled on life's path. The feminine virtues on which she had been raised for centuries: passivity, devotion, submissiveness, gentleness, proved to be fully superfluous, futile, and harmful. Harsh reality demands other characteristics from independent women: activity, resistance, determination, toughness, that is to say, characteristics which hitherto were viewed as the hallmark and privilege of men.

Robbed of the customary tutelage exercised over her by the family, woman, suddenly catapulted out of the warm nest onto the path of the struggle for existence and the class struggle, was forced to equip and arm herself with the physical characteristics possessed by the man, her comrade who is better fitted for the struggle for existence. In this hasty adjustment to the new conditions of existence, woman, quite indiscriminately, has often seized and appropriated "male rights" that upon closer scrutiny turned out to be "truths" only to the bourgeois class.

Present-day capitalist reality altogether bends its efforts, and in all possible ways, to make out of woman a type who stands incomparably closer to man than the woman of the past. This assimilation proves to be a natural and inescapable consequence of the inclusion of woman in the sphere of the economy and of social life. The capitalist world makes allowance only for women whom it succeeds in stripping of their feminine virtues and in adapting to a philosophy that hitherto belonged only to the fighter for existence, to the man.

There is no place in the ranks of those earning their own livelihood for the "unfit," that is to say, the women of the old type. Here, too, therefore, a "natural selection" among the women of the different social strata is discernible: only the stronger, more resistant disciplined natures arrive in the ranks of those "earning their own livelihood." The weak, inwardly passive, cling to the family hearth, and when the insecurity of existence tears them away from the protection of the family, to catapult them into the stream of life, supinely, they let themselves be driven by the turbid waves of legal or illegal prostitution: they enter into a marriage of convenience or they walk the streets. Those earning their own livelihood constitute a progressive army of women in which we come upon representatives of all the social strata. But the enormous majority in this army is not made up of Vera Nikodimovnas, proud of their independence, but of millions of Mathildes wrapped in grey shawls, millions of barefoot Tatianas whom poverty has driven along the new thorny path.

Those who still believe that the new "single woman" is a fruit of the heroic expenditure of energy of the strong, who assert themselves as individualities, should disabuse themselves of a gruesome error. It is not individual will, not the example of a bold Magda or a determined Renate, that created the new woman. The transformation of the feminine psyche, of its inner psychological and intellectual structure, is accomplished primarily and principally in the lower depths of society where under the scourge of hunger the adjustment of the working woman to the sharply changed conditions of existence proceeds. They, these Mathildes and Tatanias, solve no problems, they cling with all their might to the past, and only by forcibly bowing to the Lord of history, the forces of production, do they reluctantly set out on the new road. Full of sadness, cursing, or in tender nostalgia, they long to go back to the home, to the familiar warming hearth, to the quiet, modest, family joys. Oh, if only they could again leave the path, if only they could again return to the past! But the ranks of women-comrades close ever more tightly, and the feminine stream is borne ever and ever farther away from the past. Naught else is left to them save to habituate themselves to the oppressive narrowness and to arm themselves for the struggle for their place, for their right to life. A consciousness of an independent personality in the women of the working class arises and is strengthened under the rule of the "dark satanic mills," and their faith in their own power grows accordingly. The process of the accumulation of new moral and spiritual qualities in the working woman, which are indispensable for her as the representative of a definite class, proceeds consistently, inevitably, and irresistibly. But the most essential element in this process of the restructuring of woman's inner countenance affects not only individuals, but masses. The individual will drowns and disappears in the collective effort of millions of women of the working class to adjust to the new conditions of existence. Here, too, capitalism works on the broadest scale:

98

by tearing women away from the home, by wresting them away from the cradle, it transforms the submissive, passive family creatures, the obedient slaves of the husband, into a respect-demanding army of fighters for their own and general rights, for their own and general interests. The personality of the woman steels itself, grows.

But woe to the working woman who believes in the power of individual personality existing apart from others. The armored car of capital will calmly crush her. Only the serried ranks of masses of rebels can push this armored car off the path. The feeling of belongingness, the feeling of comradeship arises and strengthens itself contemporaneously with the consciousness of her personality, of her rights. A feeling that develops only weakly with the new woman of other social strata. This is that fundamental feeling, that sphere of feelings and thoughts, which draws a sharp line between single women earning their own livelihood and her sexual comrades from the bourgeoisie, those two essentially different social classes. Regardless of any difference from the woman of the past, which is the characteristic common to both, and regardless of the fact that entrance into the ranks of the working population has transformed the inner countenance of the woman in the same direction (by developing independence, strengthening personalities, broadening the mental world), women of the different social strata are driven ever farther and farther apart.

Among those earning their own livelihood the class struggle is experienced incomparably more clearly than among the women of the earlier type who scarcely knew about the inevitability of the class struggle from hearsay. For the wage earner who has crossed the family threshold in order to experience on her own person the force of social conflicts, who is forced into an active participation in the class struggle, a clear, distinct class ideology acquires the importance of a weapon in the struggle for existence. Capitalist reality draws a sharp line of demarcation between Gorky's Tatiana and Nagrodskaia's Tatiana, leading, moreover, to the fact that the woman proprietress of a workshop, ideologically, stands considerably farther from the woman worker than the "mistress," that is, the master's wife, her "good neighbor" of old. It sharpens the feeling of the social conflict among wage earners. Only one thing remains common to the women of the new type: their unique difference from the woman of the past, those specific characteristics which are the hallmark of independent single women. The latter, like the former, go through a period of rebellion, the latter, like the former, fight for the assertion of their personality, the one consciously "on principle," the other fundamentally, collectively, under the pressure of the inevitable.

But whereas with the women of the working class, the struggle for the assertion of their rights, the strengthening of their personality, coincides with the interests of the class, the women of other social strata run into unexpected obstacles: the ideology of their class is hostile to the transformation of the feminine type. In the bourgeois milieu, woman's "rebellion" bears a far sharper character, its forms are set in bolder relief, and here the psychological dramas of the new woman are far sharper, more variegated, and more complicated. Such a sharp collision between the psychology of the new woman, now in the process of formation, and class ideology does not exist in the working class and is not even possible. The new type of woman, inwardly self-reliant, independent, and free, corresponds with the morality which the working class is elaborating precisely in the interests of its class. For the working class the accomplishment of its mission does not require that she be a handmaid of the husband, an impersonal domestic creature, endowed with passive, feminine traits. Rather, it requires a personality rising and rebelling against every kind of slavery, an active, conscious, equal member of the community, of the class.

The psychology of the new, independent, single woman, according to type, is reflected in the image of the rest of her contemporaries: the traits of women, who belong to the army of those earning their own livelihood, formed by life itself, by degrees also begin to be the hallmark of the others. It matters not that those who earn their own livelihood are still in the minority, that for each one of them two, even three, women of the old type emerge. Working women set the tone of life, and form the character in respect to the image of the woman of our time.

With her transvaluation of the moral and sexual standards, the new women shake the unshakeable pillars of the souls of all the women who have not yet embarked upon the new thorny path. The dogmas that keep woman a prisoner of her own world-view lose their power over their minds. Sienkievicz's Anelka dissolves before our eyes.

The influence of women earning their own livelihood spreads far beyond their own circle. With their criticism, they "poison" the minds of their contemporaries, they smash old idols, they raise the banner of revolt against those "truths" with which women have lived for generations. By liberating themselves, the new, single women, earning their own livelihood, also liberate the passive-backward spirit, as this has been molded down the centuries, of their contemporary sisters.

Although the new woman has invaded literature, she has not yet by far supplanted the heroines of the old spiritual order, just as little as the woman-human being type has supplanted the "wifie," the "echo of the husband." Notwithstanding, we note that the characteristics and psychological traits which the new single woman has introduced are found with ever greater frequency, also, in heroines of the old type. Women novelists, who least of all set about to give us the new type, adorn their heroines unwittingly with feelings and characteristics that were not at all peculiar to the heroines of past literary periods.

Present-day literature increasingly abounds in woman-personages of the transitional type, of heroines equipped with the traits of the old and new woman alike. Moreover, a difficult process of transformation is taking place also among the woman-personages of the new type already involved in the change-effecting process: the new beginning is obstacled by the traditions and feelings of the past. The power of past centuries still weighs heavily even upon the new, free woman. Atavistic feelings interrupt and weaken the new experiences, outlived conceptions still hold the feminine mind thrusting towards freedom in their clutches.

The old and the new struggle in the souls of women, in permanent enmity. Contemporary heroines, therefore, must wage a struggle on two fronts: with the external world and with the inclinations of their grandmothers dwelling in the recesses of their beings.

"The new ideas are already born in us," says Hedwig Dohn,

"but the old have not yet died out, the experiences of past generations still sit solidly in us, even though we already possess the intellect of the new woman, her will power."

The transformation of the feminine psyche, which is adjusted to the new conditions of its economic and social existence, will not be achieved without a strong, dramatic self-overcoming. Every step in this direction creates collisions which were utterly unknown to the heroines of the past. And these conflicts, which take place in the souls of women, by degrees begin to draw the attention of novelists, begin to serve as sources of artistic inspiration. Woman, by degrees, is being transformed from an object of tragedy of the male soul into the subject of an independent tragedy.

AFTERWORD
BY IRING FETSCHER

*"I still remember how gaily and how long he
laughed when somewhere he read Martov's ut-
terance, 'There are only two communists in
Russia, Lenin and Mme. Kollontai.'"*

MAXIM GORKI, Reminiscences of My Youth

Most of the important women among the Marxist revolutionaries came from the upper class. Presumably the oppression of woman in the petty bourgeoisie and proletariat was so complete there that barely one of them managed to free herself from the co-ercions of inherited thought and behavioral patterns. The Krups-kayas, Luxemburgs, Balabanovs, Kollontais spoke as the repre-sentatives of the millions of women from the rural and industrial proletariat who were not yet able to speak in their own name. But this also means that the origin of their option for socialism and the revolution lay in a consciousness of social responsibility, indeed of sympathy for the sufferings of the lower strata of the population. Alexandra Kollontai herself reports it in her auto-biography. Elsewhere she has noted, "Since childhood I liked the 'all goes well with me' feeling. The consciousness that 'all goes well with me' but that, at the same time, others must suffer distress . . . grieved me enormously. I pace from one corner of the room to the other and torment myself with the thought: how can one so arrange the scheme of things so that 'all goes well' with everybody?" (*Itkina,* page 8). As today with many revolutionary intellectuals of bourgeois families in Latin Amer-ica, in the case of Alexandra Kollontai it was through servants that she first experienced the sufferings of the lower classes. The news that one of the family's servants had died because he had gone home in a flimsy blouse, after having sweated over a par-ticularly strenuous chore, shook her deeply and forever destroyed the harmony in which she had been growing up till then. There-fore the political enlightenment that had been doled out to her by the house tutoress Strakova fell upon fertile ground. Alexandra Kollontai did not confine herself to compassion but bestirred herself to learn the magnitude and the causes of the suffering of the proletariat and—soon after graduating from the university—she decided to join the working-class movement. Nevertheless for her, as for Rosa Luxemburg, the origin of her option for socialism never lost its importance. She never lost sight of the liberation of each and every individual member thereof. In contrast to Lenin or Trotsky, in her pre-diplomatic phase, she probably lacked the sense for power and the political ability to proceed along circuitous paths leading to the seizure and maintenance of power. Her adhesion to the Workers' Opposition (1921), as well as her insistence upon women's liberation, are to be understood as the expression of an unbroken emancipatory idealism which could not always adjust itself to external circumstances. Nevertheless her activity yielded abundant fruit, above all in its third phase, the phase of her diplomatic representation in Oslo, Mexico, and Stockholm. When she died in Moscow in 1952 loneliness, of course, had closed in around her. A. M. Itkina describes a visit to her in the autumn of 1946: "The eyes, in which sadness lay hidden, looked friendly and concentrated. I felt that she was not in good spirits: in this time of repressions based upon unsubstantiated charges she had experienced the ruin of close friends and comrades" (pp. 125f.). Two former husbands of Alexandra Kollontai also belonged to the close friends and comrades whose names Mme. Itkina, prudently, does not mention: the legendary commander of the Red Fleet Pavel Dybenko with whom together they had formed "the most famous pair of lovers of the October Revolution," and the leader of the Workers' Opposition, Alexander Shylapnikov, whose cause she so passionately defended at the Tenth Party Congress. Both perished during the Stalinist "purges."

A similar note is discernible in the report of the chairwoman of the Finnish-Soviet Society, Mme. Sylvi Kyllikki-Kilpi, who, along with the Finnish ambassador, visited Alexandra Kollontai in 1947: "One evening we went to her flat which she shared with an old friend from Sweden, who was both her lady companion and nurse. Madame Kollontai could not move since she was paralyzed. Although the flat was spacious it gave the impression of being small and cramped because it was cluttered with old pieces of furniture, photographs, and mementoes. Madame Kollontai sat in the same enormous chair throughout the interview. We spoke Swedish in which she was very fluent. Her conversation was vivacious. She was wearing a beautiful dress with a laced collar and lots of expensive jewelry. She no longer recalled that slender, enchanting young agitator [as Frau Kilpi had known Alexandra Kollontai in her childhood—I.F.] . . . but she still had lots of charm. One could see that she had been very beautiful in her youth. Madame Kollontai complained a bit about loneliness, only a few old friends were still alive, she could no longer keep up a correspondence with friends abroad" (cited from a report in the Finnish periodical *Anna,* no. 9, March 3, 1970). The Finnish people and the Finnish Government gratefully remember Alexandra Kollontai because the major share of the credit for the signing of the armistice and peace between Finland and the Soviet Union is due to her. She is also credited with advising Lenin on questions relating to Finland already in 1917–18 and with convincing him of the necessity of granting independence to Finland.

Three high points in the life of Alexandra Kollontai should be set into bolder relief, as she herself has done in her autobiographical sketch: her theoretical considerations on the emancipation of women and of sexual life under socialism, her argumentation in the name of the Workers' Opposition against NEP (the "New Economic Policy") and the increasing bureaucraticism in the Soviet Union (1921–22), and, finally, her diplomatic activity.

Almost all of the passages in which she speaks of women's emancipation belong to the sections of the autobiography that fell victim to the author's self-critical pencil. But even that which has again become visible through our reconstruction remains far behind that which she expressed in speeches and writings at the beginning of the 1920's. Above all she hardly mentions her conception of the "new morality" with respect to sexual relations which, among others, she developed in great detail in her book *The New Morality and the Working Class*. It is, of course, no accident that it was in the phase of the burgeoning Stalinization that precisely such concepts as women's liberation and sexual emancipation were shoved into the background. With the "conservative" turn of Soviet pedagogy (against the opposition of Nadezhda Krupskaya, Lenin's widow), of Soviet family law and the turn to "authoritarian" communism, all the efforts to which Alexandra Kollontai, up to then, had given her main attention were bound to be viewed as "undesirable." The desperate struggle for democracy and freedom of opinion which she waged in the ranks of the Workers' Opposition also was connected with this development, which she had foreseen and rejected. A development which had already begun with Lenin and Trotsky, however, was first dogmatized and schematized under Stalin.

Whereas most of the leading Bolsheviks entertained conservative, if not out and out puritan, views in questions of sexual morality, Alexandra Kollontai exhibited a freer and less inhibited attitude in her theoretical writings and fiction as well as in her personal life-style. This unconventional attitude together with her proverbial beauty and elegance gave rise to many legends and slanders among her enemies and followers alike. Unconsciously expressed in them is the repressed sexuality of the slanderers, their frustration and their discontent. According to the most famous legend, Alexandra Kollontai is supposed to have declared that sexual contacts were matters as simple and as unproblematic as drinking a glass of water. Lenin campaigns against this theory in a conversation with Clara Zetkin which she has preserved in her *Reminiscences of Lenin*. To be sure, Lenin does not mention Comrade Kollontai by name, but presumably he too identified her with this "theory." According to Clara Zetkin, Lenin, at that time, had disapprovingly declared, "The changed attitude of the young people to questions of sexual life is of course based on a 'principle' and a theory. Many of them call their attitude 'revolutionary' and 'communistic.' And they honestly believe that it is so. That does not impress us old people. Although I am nothing but a gloomy ascetic, the so-called 'new sexual life' of the youth—and sometimes of the old—often seems to me to be purely bourgeois, an extension of bourgeois brothels. That has nothing whatever in common with freedom of love as we communists understand it. You must be aware of the famous theory that in communist society the satisfaction of sexual desires, of love, will be as simple and unimportant as drinking a glass of water. This glass-of-water theory has made our young people mad, quite mad. It has proved fatal to many young boys and girls. Its adherents maintain that it is Marxist. But thanks for such Marxism which directly and immediately attributes all phenomena and changes in the ideological superstructure of society to its economic basis

. . . I think this glass-of-water theory is completely un-Marxist and, moreover, anti-social. In sexual love there is not only simple nature to be considered, but also cultural circumstances, whether they are of a high or low order. In his *Origin of the Family* Engels showed how significant is the development and refinement of the general sex urge into individual sex love. The relations of the sexes to each other are not simply an expression of the play of forces between the economics of society and a physical need, isolated in thought by study from the physiological aspect . . . Of course, thirst must be satisfied. But will the normal man in normal circumstances lie down in the gutter and drink out of a puddle, or out of a glass with a rim greasy from many lips? But the social aspect is most important of all. Drinking water is of course an individual affair. But in love two lives are concerned, and a third, a new life arises. It is that which gives it its social interest, which gives rise to a duty towards the community."

Lenin himself must have probably felt that this sermon had an overly conservative ring because finally he adds, "I don't mean to preach asceticism by my criticism. Not in the least. Communism will not bring asceticism, but joy of life, power of life, and a satisfied love life will help to do that. But in my opinion the present widespread hypertrophy in sexual matters does not give joy and force to life, but takes it away. In the age of revolution that is bad, very bad.

"Young people, particularly, need the joy and force of life. Healthy sport, swimming, racing, walking, bodily exercises of every kind, and many-sided intellectual interests. Learning, studying, inquiry as far as possible in common. That will give young people more than eternal theories and discussions about sexual

112

problems and so-called 'living to the full.' Healthy bodies, healthy minds! Neither monk nor Don Juan, nor the intermediate attitude of the German philistine." The reference to lectures and discussions on sexual problems could have also been aimed at Alexandra Kollontai.

If we search for the precise place in which Alexandra Kollontai assertedly propagated such a radical and mindless theory of sexual enjoyment, we come upon the character of Genia in her novel *Great Love*. Lenin's critical observations on the attitude of many young people of his time, as expressed in the conversation with Clara Zetkin, partly apply to her. Alexandra Kollontai portrays Genia without a moralizing criticism, but by no means as a clear ideal. She lets Genia make the following observation: "I suppose you disapprove, like mother, because I give myself without falling in love. But one must have time to fall in love. I have read novels and I know how love takes possession of one's faculties to the exclusion of everything else. But I have no time. Our activity in the district has taken hold of us all so completely that none of us has had time to think of anything else, of personal matters. We run from one task to another. There are times when there is little else to do . . . time enough to notice that this one or that is a little more attractive than the rest. But before it can become more than a passing fancy, we are off again, to new work. We never get beyond the first stages of comradely affection. This one is called to the front, that one is sent away. New excitement, new impressions, and we forget. So we simply take advantage of the few short hours of release that are granted to us—there is nothing binding, no responsibility . . . Of course, there is always the danger of contracting disease. But no man will lie to you about that—no comrade, that is—if you look straight into his eyes and ask for the truth."

The same Genia, who gives herself to men without loving them, is altogether capable of love, however, as she herself says. For example, she loves her mother: "My mother. There is no one like her. In a sense, she is more to me than Lenin. There is something about her . . . don't believe I could live without her. Her happiness means more to me than anything else in the world, . . . no, I will never love as mother loved . . . How can one work, if one loses oneself like that?" The narrator leaves open the question as to whether the future will show "that the new class, the new youth with its new experiences and its new conceptions and feelings, is on the road to happiness," or how the phenomenon should be judged otherwise. Her theoretical works clearly indicate that she judged this radical, emancipated attitude in a positive sense, even though she personally was not yet able to accept it.

In the chapter "The New Woman" of her book *The New Morality and the Working Class* she gives an account of a fifth —up to now unknown type of heroine—"with independent demands on life, heroines who assert their personality, heroines who protest against the universal servitude of woman in the State, the family, society, who fight for their rights as representatives of their sex." For these emancipated women artists or women scientists feeling is no longer all-dominant, at all events the feeling of absolute submission to love for a man no longer takes top priority. At the center of her life stands her own work, her own accomplishment, and the self-consciousness that grows out of it: "The new women do not want exclusive possession when they love. Since they demand respect for the freedom of their own feeling, they learn to accord this respect to others. Characteristic of this is the attitude of the heroine towards the rival as portrayed in a string of contemporary novels. We come upon tactful, circumspect behavior towards the other woman rather than defamatory attacks . . ." "In the new woman the human being increasingly triumphs over the jealous 'wifie.' Thereby the character of inter-personal relations changes. The woman ceases to understand herself primarily, or even exclusively, as a 'sexual object.' She demands respect and recognition not so much as 'wifie' but as 'I,' as an independent personality. The new woman forgives an affront to the 'wifie' in her, but she never forgets the least inattentiveness to her personality." Obviously here too Alexandra Kollontai had taken her own world of experience as a standard for interpretation inasmuch as a little later she writes, "These increased demands upon the man are the warrant for the fact that so many heroines of modern novels rush from one enjoyment to another, from one love to the other in the wearying search for their ideal: harmony between passion and spiritual kinship, the reconciliation of love and freedom, comradeship with mutual independence." This corresponds pretty much with Alexandra Kollontai's portrayal of her life-experiences in her autobiography where she states that "young women are learning today, that work and the longing for love can be harmoniously combined." Presumably so is the assertion, "the woman of the present feels in marriage a fetter, even when no outer, formal bond exists. The psyche of the old human being that still lives in us, creates moral fetters in us incomparably stronger than the outer ones," such statements belong to those which begat the slanders flung at Mme. Kollontai by conservative males in the bourgeois and proletarian camps alike. In her view, liberation from these "moral fetters," which threaten inner freedom and independence, belongs most decisively to that emancipation which will be made possible by the socialistic order of society. In numerous modern novels in 1920 she found that the struggle of young women no longer revolved around the right to love, but around "A protest against moral imprisonment, even that of the outwardly freest feeling." She views this struggle as a phenomenon of transition and believes that in the future it would be possible to combine "inner freedom and independence with the all-consuming passion of love." First of all, of course, emancipation consists in the fact that "the heroines of contemporary novels . . . transgress limits of the usual sexual code of virtue" and nevertheless—as has been the case with men since time immemorial—they successfully lay claim to the reader's respect and approval. "Contemporary heroines become mothers without being married, they leave husbands or beloved, their lives can be rich in love-experiences and, notwithstanding, they will count themselves among 'forlorn creatures' as little as will the author of the modern reader." Finally she summarizes her sketch of the "new woman" as follows: "Self-discipline instead of emotional rapture, a capacity to value her own freedom and independence instead of impersonal submissiveness; the assertion of her own individuality instead of the naïve effort to internalize and reflect the alien image of the 'beloved.' The display of the right to family happiness instead of the hypocritical mask of virginity, finally the assignation of love-experiences to a subordinate place in life. Before us no longer stands the 'wifie,' the shadow of the husband—before us stands the personality, the woman as human being."

Alexandra Kollontai awaits the generalization of this new type of woman from the process of capitalist industrialization and the socialist revolution which it made possible: "Here, too, capitalism works on the broadest scale: by tearing women away from the home, by wresting them away from the cradle, it transforms the submissive, passive family creatures, the obedient female slaves of the husbands, into a respect-demanding army of fighters for their own and general rights, for their own and general interests. The personality of the woman steels itself, grows." The experience of the last fifty years confirms the fact that this development obviously has not continued, although the process of drawing women into the process of production has by no means been interrupted. Alexandra Kollontai believes that in the proletariat the struggle for the emancipation of woman's personality merges with the struggle for the political emancipation of the class, whereas in the bourgeoisie it perforce leads to conflict with bourgeois class interests: "The ideology of their class is hostile to the transformation of the feminine type. In the bourgeois milieu woman's 'rebellion' bears a far sharper character, its forms are set in bolder relief, and here the psychological dramas of the new woman are far sharper, more variegated and more complicated. Such a sharp collision between the psychology of the new woman, now in the process of formation, and class ideology does not exist in the working class and is not even possible. The new type of woman, inwardly self-reliant, independent, and free, corresponds with the morality which the working class is elaborating precisely in the interests of its class. For the working class the accomplishment of its mission does not require that she be a handmaid of the husband, an impersonal domestic creature, endowed with passive, feminine traits Rather it requires a personality rising and rebelling against

117

every kind of slavery, an active, conscious, equal member of the community, of the class." The "bourgeoisification" of the industrial proletariat and the restoration of petty bourgeois moral standards in the communist states have most successfully worked together—and fatefully with respect to the emancipation of women and workers alike—to bring the development discerned by Alexandra Kollontai to a standstill or even to annul it. In the highly developed industrialized Western societies, consumer-goods advertising has essentially contributed to fixing woman's image as an expensive "luxury article" and this fact itself subliminally conduces to an acceptation of the authoritarian-male cliché which Alexandra Kollontai fancied had been overcome long ago. In countries such as the Soviet Union, the bureaucratic power apparatus and the strengthening of the "family structure" with its still prevalently male authority figures has restored the petty bourgeois code under the banner of "moral health" and superiority vis-à-vis the "decadent West." The reactionary conception of woman's role which has become visible on the basis of Stalin's private utterances and the product of his education—Svetlana—is merely a prominent confirmation of the behavior model which he neither created nor perpetuated by himself. What was lost on the way to the "bourgeoisification" of the proletarian consciousness—male as well as female—was above all the "feeling of belongingness, the feeling of comradeship" which Alexandra Kollontai rightly defined as "that fundamental feeling which draws a sharp line between single women earning their own livelihood and their sexual comrades from the bourgeoisie." As wage-earners and consumers, isolated just as much as candidates for the favor of (rich?) men, women cannot emancipate themselves no matter how much of their clothes they may shed. Alexandra Kollontai's writings are positively chaste compared with the sexual exhibitionism that nowadays is wrongly confused with emancipation and freedom. But for this very reason there is also an absolute earnestness and a determined orientation towards a real liberation.

Alexandra Kollontai describes the "sexual crisis" of our century in the last chapter of her book, "Sexual Relations and Class Struggle." In it we find formulations that have completely preserved their actuality. "We humans, belonging to the century of the sharpest class conflicts and of an individualist morality, still suffer from an inescapable spiritual loneliness. This loneliness in the midst of big, bustling cities with their variegated enticements, even among the crowd of close friends and fellow travellers, arouses in the individual of our day a pathological greed to cling to the illusion of a 'kindred soul,' a soul, of course, which belongs to a being of the opposite sex, for only cunning Eros is able—at least fleetingly—to expel the darkness of loneliness."

From this utter panic fear or loneliness grows an exorbitant demand for love, a psychical greed for possession which, at the same time, represents an internalization of the bourgeois concept of property. The poverty "in love potencies" (Meisel-Hess) from which both sexes suffer, leaves each one to strive exclusively to obtain "from the other the greatest possible measure in spiritual and physical enjoyments for oneself," a form of love doomed to failure, as Jean-Paul Sartre has rightly shown. In the criticism of egoistic individualism in love it becomes clear how Alexandra Kollontai pictures spiritual relations between the sexes in a future society. "We lay claim always to the whole personality of our 'contracting party in love,' yet at the same time we are not capable of observing the simplest rule of love: to meet the soul of the other with the most tender attentiveness. We are gradually being taught the formula by the new relations between the sexes, observable here and there, which rest upon two new principles: the principle of full freedom and that of equality and sincerity of comradely solidarity . . ."

Alexandra Kollontai does not expect the "sexual crisis of the present" to be overcome more easily by the spread of matrimonial-like bonds susceptible of easier dissolution, or by other changes effected within the framework of the existing social order, but exclusively by the socialist revolution. The preconditions for the solution of this crisis would mature in a socialist society which ends the shackling of all women to the household, which abolishes the distinction between legitimate and illegitimate children, and which extends its full protection to the expectant mother. Above all a "fundamental restructuring of our psyche" would take place which, once emancipated from all the egoistic and individualistic behavior-models, for the first time would be capable of true love. Nevertheless she considers that one of the present and pressing tasks of the revolutionary working class and its Party is "to create healthier and more joyous relations between the sexes," and to work out the new "sexual morality of the working class." The ideas that Alexandra Kollontai sketched out exactly fifty years ago have no longer been elaborated upon further since that time. Five or six years later the turn to petty bourgeoisdom in Soviet communism was already clearly perceptible. Yet rather than re-signing herself to it, Alexandra Kollontai put her great rhetorical gifts at the service of the Workers' Opposition which belonged to the inner-Party groups and which, since 1921, had been attempting to divert the Communist Party from the path of bureaucratism and the formation of a new class.

At the Tenth Party Congress of the Russian Communist Party (Bolshevik), Alexandra Kollontai delivered a comprehensive report in which she passionately defended the position of the Workers' Opposition, to which the leader of the Metal Workers Union as well as the chairmen of the central committee of the Mine Workers and the Textile Workers belonged. She asserted that the voice of the Workers' Opposition was the class voice of the Russian industrial proletariat, which was registering its criticism with the Party apparatus. "The higher we climb up the ladder of Soviet and Party 'posts,' the fewer followers of the Opposition do we find. The deeper one penetrates into the masses, the stronger is the response one finds to the program of the Workers' Opposition." "The Workers' Opposition is, therefore, the progressive segment of the proletariat which has not broken the living bond with the worker-masses organized in trade unions and has not spread itself over Soviet institutions."

The substance of the struggle, on the one hand, is the demand for collective leadership in plant management and in the State, for more worker democracy, and, on the other hand, a criticism of the concessions which the New Economic Policy was making to peasants, traders, and foreign investors. The Workers' Opposition feared not only the elimination of democracy, but also the demolition of the socialistic organization of property. "A one-man management [which had been introduced in all plants and factories in 1930—I. F.] is of one piece with the individualistic world-view of the bourgeois class. A one-man management, that is, one cut off from the collective, the 'free,' isolated will of the individual which appears in all sectors beginning with the recognition of an autocratic State head up to the absolute rule of a factory manager, is the highest wisdom of bourgeois thought. The bourgeoisie does not believe in the power of the collective. It loves only 'to drive the mass together into an obedient herd' . . . and to stampede this herd according to its . . . self-glorifying will whither the leader fancies it be necessary." In a socialist society, however, Alexandra Kollontai asserts, collective bodies of the working class should direct "social-productive labor." The Party, however, advocates a governmental directive body and therein she discerns a "serious crisis for our Party." Alexandra Kollontai attributes the cause of the differences of opinion between the Party leadership and the Workers' Opposition to the difficult historical circumstances and the economic backwardness of Russia at the moment of the Revolution, both of which factors made it extraordinarily difficult to realize the program. Under these circumstances it was, perhaps, inevitable that "specialists" in all possible areas would be accepted into the Party and State apparatus to which they brought with them their bourgeois and petty bourgeois views and, assertedly, had begun to influence the Party leadership itself. Thus military specialists had brought "the spirit of the past into the Red Army (officer discipline, epaulettes, decorations, blind subordination, and, instead of class discipline, the arbitrary will of the supreme Commander, etc.)." But these influences become particularly dangerous when they are extended to the sphere of the economy, to the sphere of economic construction and of economic self-administration: "Production is *their* organization. That is the essence of communism. To keep workers away from the organization of production, to deprive them . . . of the opportunity to develop their creative capacities in production, in the organization of new economic forms and, instead, to trust in the 'know how' of specialists . . . means to abandon the path of scientific Marxist thinking. But precisely that is what the heads of our Party are doing at the moment. In view of the utterly disastrous state of our economy . . . the heads of our Party, gripped by a lack of faith in the creative capabilities of the worker-collective, seek for salvation from the economic chaos . . . in the descendants of the bourgeois-capitalist past, in business people and technicians. They are the ones who give rise to the laughable naïve belief that communism can be introduced in a bureaucratic way."

Alexandra Kollontai's whole argumentation winds up with the conclusion that the construction of the new society should be handed over to the trade unions as the genuine organ of the proletarian class-dictatorship—not to the Party since it tacks—and up to a certain degree must steer—between the different social classes: peasantry, petty bourgeoisie, proletariat, and "specialists." The assumption of the direction of the economy by bureaucratic State or Party bodies, however, has immediately perceptible consequences for the workers. Thus, for example, questions of healthful conditions on the job, the improvement of working conditions, of the housing situation, and so on, always occupy last place. Indeed, a plan for the reorganization of housing has not even been started. Also "the growing inequality between the privileged group of the population of Soviet Russia and the ordinary workers, the 'backbone of the dictatorship' of the proletariat, sharpens and increases the growing discontent."

In the view of Alexandra Kollontai and the Workers' Opposition, however, these concrete abuses, which they pointed out are not denied even by the Party leadership, are jointly and severally consequences of bureaucratization and of the infiltration of "non-proletarian" elements into the Party. Accordingly, she demands a Party purge, to which the non-proletarians who joined after the Revolution are to be subjected. Above all, however, the direction and management of production must be handed over to the All Russian Congress of Trade Unions which is to elect a central body, while the workers of each individual plant must elect and control their directors. In opposition to both Trotsky and Lenin, who had spoken of an educational process as a necessary prior step to workers' self-administration, Madame Kollontai objects that a modern, practice-related education can ensue only for the activity of the top-level managers of the economy themselves. And she compares the "moderate" position of Nikolai Bukharin, who wanted to give workers at least a limited right to participate in management in questions not related to production, with those "pedagogues who impart instruction according to the old system to this day—in exchange for which, however, they spur the pupils to elect the committee chairman in the class, in the canteen, and for dramatic recitals, etc." In the place of such sand-box democracy for the working class, the Workers' Opposition demands a real participation of the workers in economic self-administration and in the organization of production. "The Party can train a Red Army man, a political functionary, people in general to solve already formulated tasks. But the Party cannot train any builder of the communist economy—this requires pro-ductive-constructive work within the frame of the trade unions." The criticism directed at the Party leadership crops up repeatedly; it is charged with having lost faith in the working masses and instead having placed it in "specialists" stemming from the bourgeoisie. It is here that the Workers' Opposition discerns the

124

major mistake of the leadership—especially of Lenin and Trotsky. Theoretically the dispute revolves around the question: which organization could most rightly claim to represent the class of the industrial proletariat? The trade unions, asserts Alexandra Kollontai. "The revolution can be carried out by the vanguard of the class [that is, the Party—I.F.], but the economic foundation of the rule of the new society can be created only by the whole class in the practical day-to-day work of their most important class collective [the trade unions—I.F.]. Kollontai argues wholly in the spirit of Rosa Luxemburg when she proclaims, "We cannot decree communism. It can be created only through active searching, through temporary setbacks but, at all events, through the creative force of the working class itself."

The demand set forth by the Workers' Opposition may, in fact, have been impossible of fulfillment in 1921. The widespread demoralization of the whole population was the result of a year-long famine, the weakening of the proletariat by the shutting down of numerous plants and by the fact that workers were streaming back to their families in the countryside. All this may have made direct participation by the workers in the management of the economy and in building of the economy, as demanded by Alexandra Kollontai, impossible at that time. Nevertheless her warning retains merit in terms of theory. She had opportunely pointed to the dangers that were to manifest their full dimensions only much later: the swiftly growing bureaucracy, the waning of democratic life, the restriction on freedom of discussion—even within the Party itself: "The essence of bureaucratism, its harmfulness, does not lie only in red tape . . . but in the fact that all questions are decided not by exchanges of opinions, not by the active, direct initiative of the interested persons, but in a formal way 'from above', by an individual, or, at best, by an extremely restricted collegium in which the interested persons often are not at all represented." "The fear of criticism and freedom of thought which is bound up with the system of bureaucratism at times assumes farcical features with us. What self-initiative has ever existed without freedom of opinion and thought? . . . We fear the self-initiative of the masses, we fear to give full scope to the creative activity of the class, we fear any and all criticism, we have ceased to trust the masses—this is the source of our entire bureaucratism.

Alexandra Kollontai, in the name of the Workers' Opposition, proposes a Party purge, above all, however, the restoration of the principle of election. "Nomination," she complains, has become a general, recognized, legitimate phenomenon. The practice of nomination creates an unhealthy atmosphere in the Party because it disturbs equality and comradeship, it fosters careerism, abets nepotism . . . deepens the cleavage between the "heads" and the "lower levels." "Freedom of opinion and discussion, the right to criticism within the Party and among members of the trade unions," is as necessary as the election and recall of all function-aries.

Similar demands, moreover, as she points out, have been set forth by other groups within the Party (for example, by the Moscow Committee of the Russian Communist Party). Unfortunately, however, one is forced to note that even the resolution of the Party Conference of 1920 which provided that in the future nominations were to be replaced by simple recommendation was not carried out in practice. Many young comrades, however, would find such Party practices repellent.

With the development of bureaucratism, authoritarian-minded-

126

ness and the cult of the functionary are spreading in the Party, she continues. What is particularly noteworthy here is that the critical observation was made as early as 1921, at a time, that is to say, when the modest and inconspicuous model of the Party leader, as embodied by Lenin, still determined Party life and practice—and Stalin was only one leading functionary among many. There is no doubt that the Stalin cult was a product of the bureaucratic power system, and that Stalin was not the creator of Soviet bureaucratism, as acknowledged by the official "theory" of the epoch of the cult of personality.

Despite the sharp words that Lenin and Trotsky flung at the operators of the Workers' Opposition, at that time neither Shylapnikov nor Kollontai were expelled from the Party. Lenin viewed the Workers' Opposition as "a petty bourgeois anarchist element hiding behind the back of the proletariat" (Lenin, Tenth Party Congress). At the instigation of both Lenin and Trotsky, criticism of the leading role of the Party was most sharply condemned. The resolution of the Party Congress "on syndicalist and anarchist deviations" states, "Marxism taught—and this teaching is confirmed by the whole experience of our revolution—that only the political party of the working class, that is, the Communist Party, is able to unite, educate, and organize a vanguard of the proletariat and of all working masses that is capable of counteracting the inevitable petty bourgeois waverings of the masses, the traditions and the inevitable backsliding of the proletariat into trade-unionist narrowness or trade-unionist prejudices and of leading, on an all-around basis, the proletarian movement and, consequently, all the working masses. Without this the dictatorship of the proletariat is meaningless."

Even sharper was the tone of Trotsky's speech. He argued,

"The Workers' Opposition has come out with dangerous slogans. They have made a fetish of democratic principles. They have placed the workers' right to elect representatives above the Party, as it were, as if the Party were not entitled to assert *its* [sic] *dictatorship* [my emphasis—I.F.], even if this dictatorship temporarily clashed with the passing moods of the workers' democracy ... It is necessary to create among us the awareness of the revolutionary historical birthright of the party. The party is obliged to maintain its dictatorship, regardless of temporary wavering in the spontaneous moods of the masses, regardless of the temporary vacillations even in the working class ... The dictatorship does not base itself at every given moment on the formal principle of a workers' democracy, although the workers' democracy is, of course, the only method by which the masses can be drawn more and more into political life" (Isaac Deutscher, *The Prophet Armed; Trotsky: 1879–1921,* Vintage Books, pp. 508–509). Alexandra was as little disposed to admit defeat after the Tenth Party Congress as were other members of the Workers' Opposition. At the Third Congress of the Comintern—July 5, 1921—and on the 65th birthday of Clara Zetkin to whom she was bound by lifelong friendship, she spoke once more in the name of the Workers' Opposition. Again she attacked the concessions of the New Economic Policy which "rob the working class of its faith in communism," and she criticised the Party leadership for lacking faith in the creative force of the proletariat. She deliberately brought the inner-Russian quarrel before the international forum because she believed that it rested on questions of principle which concerned the *whole* working-class movement. "But even if we should temporarily save production in Russia [with the bureaucratic methods then being offered—I.F.] there accordingly exists the

128

great danger that at the same time we shall thereby lose the trust of the working masses in our Party. Consequently we believe that one should by no means take a sympathetic attitude towards the policy, as we see so many comrades doing. On the contrary, we should deal critically with this policy so that the comrades in countries that are still capitalist can draw a lesson therefrom. The only thing which can save us is to have a strong core in our Party which stands up for our old, solid principles, which will be at hand at the moment when the Revolution breaks out among you. And if the turn in the whole Soviet policy continues further [the development towards a bureaucratic State capitalism—I.F.] and if out of our communist Republic a non-communist and a merely Soviet Republic is created, then this core of solid communists will be there to seize the red banner of the Revolution and to help communism to victory all over the world." (Minutes of the Third Congress). Once more Trotsky took the plan to refute Alexandra Kollontai's theses. He did so with a blend of irony and rhetorical pungency. In an introductory remark he faults Alexandra Kollontai for having registered her name on the speakers' list on her own: "I don't know, perhaps it also belongs to the question of concessions that one wants to appear somewhat exaggeratedly chivalrous—in this case I do not know the German expression—perhaps Amazon-like . . . (Radek: Walküre-like), Walküre-like, I leave the responsibility for this expression to Comrade Radek (merriment), because Comrade Kollontai has entered her name on the speakers' list, whereas with us it is customary to deal with the question in the Buro, in the Central Committee. One has found it wholly normal that a tiny minority, politically hardly worthy of consideration with respect to the question, desires to bring its shading, its tendency, to the notice of the international Congress" (*op. cit.*, p. 785). Only several years later, of course, Trotsky himself was to feel it necessary to appeal to the International to act as arbiter between him and the Stalinist leadership. Here he still expressly concedes that Alexandra Kollontai had the right ("it is her good right") to take the floor, but at the same time he tries to belittle the importance of the Workers' Opposition. Essentially, he levels two arguments against the Workers' Opposition. On the one hand, he criticizes the "metaphysical conception" of Alexandra Kollontai who believes "that the capitalist system has outlived itself" and that, therefore, it is no longer possible "to borrow from this system" something that is to the advantage of the Soviet Union (pp. 785f.). Thereupon he carries this position *ad absurdum* by showing how trade with the capitalist States almost imperceptibly turns into concessions to foreign enterprises which at the same time—in view of the urgent need for machines and tools— could be advantageous to the Soviet Union. Ironically, he notes, "Therefore I would like very much to know where Comrade Kollontai's principled opposition begins and where it ends, with the purchase of [capitalist—I.F.] locomotives, with the payment with gold, with the payment with wood, or with the payment of wood in the form of a forest. I am afraid that the opposition begins first with the felling of the forest" (p. 787). On the other hand, Trotsky tries to prove that the requisition of specialists in the military as well as the economic field is indispensable and in no way calls into question the leading role of the working class. On the contrary, precisely because the working class (through the Party) has seized power, it can requisition specialists which it still needs temporarily for individual tasks without impairment to its rule. In none of the two cases—either with the concessions

130

to foreign entrepreneurs or with the requisition of bourgeois specialists—is it proper to speak of a "lack of trust in the force of the Russian working class, of the Russian proletariat" (p. 789). Rather, Trotsky continues, such an attitude is found among the members of the Workers' Opposition. It is difficult to determine whether Trotsky here intentionally, or actually, misunderstands Alexandra Kollontai. Her objection was not directed against the requisition of specialists but against the infiltration of the apparatus and against the transformation of the political as well as the economic organizations into bureaucratic bodies. In no way could the objection be invalidated by reference to the indispensability of specialists. Indeed in an interruption Alexandra Kollontai protests against drawing *technicians* into the discussion. To be sure, she was not given the opportunity to make a point-by-point rebuttal to Trotsky's criticism, but this was done by Hempel of the K.A.P.D., the Communist Workers Party of Germany, which espoused views similar to those of the Workers' Opposition.

According to Hempel, the question of over-riding importance was that "for Germany and Western Europe another conception of Party dictatorship" is required than that obtaining in Russia where probably, in consequence of the country's backwardness, especially rigid and centralistic forms of dictatorship might have been unavoidable. If, however, democratic forces begin to stir within the Russian proletariat, this is of importance to the International and "we should support these aspirations. Account must be taken of this pressure from below," for here lies a force that "sustains the proletarian dictatorship better than foreign capital." Nikolai Bukharin, whose job obviously was to deliver the *coup de grace* to the Opposition, refers sarcastically to the Kronstadt rebellion which is sometimes "confused with this movement from below." In reply to Alexandra Kollontai's argument Bukarin declares, "After all, we cannot really view manipulations with creative power, with the spirit of mechanics as a real argument, and content ourselves with that. Comrade Gorter in his very famous pamphlet says that the world is going to the dogs because the Russian comrades do not hold to the historic-materialist standpoint. Now we understand what historical materialism is. It is the historical materialism of Comrade Kollontai who has spoken very much about the spirit of creation and matters of that kind, about the spirit that cares not a fig for base material conditions and mechanical representation that Comrade Lenin has mentioned here. Therefore, I say, that what is most lacking in Comrade Kollontai's whole speech is that nobody can understand just what she is actually proposing . . ." Summarizing the speeches of Kollontai and Hempel, Bukarin concludes, "Generally speaking, I must establish that the whole criticism that has been directed against us was not criticism but mere phraseology." Lenin, to whom the chairman gave the floor so that he could make the concluding summary, contents himself with the remark, "Comrades, I am in complete agreement [with that] which my friend Bukharin has said. I have nothing to add and therefore decline to make a concluding summary." Perhaps it was an impulse of chivalry towards the old comrade-in-arms which induced him to refrain from participating in the critical judgment passed upon her. At the Eleventh Party Congress of the Russian Communist Party in March of 1922, Alexandra Kollontai once more espoused the cause of the workers' democracy. Vainly she tried to induce the Party leadership—basing herself on a resolution of the Tenth Party Congress—to strengthen democracy within the working-class movement. "Our solution lies in the creativity of the working masses" (Minutes of the Eleventh Party Congress, Moscow, 1936). She withdrew from the inner-Party opposition only after Lenin's death when the triumvirs, more and more forcibly and decisively, were demanding discipline and unanimity within the Party. At that time Zinoviev, in a reference to Alexandra Kollontai and Shylapnikov, declared, "Every criticism of the party line, even a so-called 'left' criticism, is now objectively a Menshevik criticism." He went even further and declared that such a criticism was indeed more obnoxious than that of the Mensheviks. Thereby inner Party criticism was made into a punishable offense—something which had never happened in Lenin's time no matter how vehement the polemics.

There are no detailed reports of Kollontai's withdrawal from the Opposition and her entry into diplomatic service. A. M. Itkina merely notes, "Finally she joined Lenin again." She was sent to her first post abroad already in the autumn of 1922—as a legation counsellor to the trade mission that was to be newly established in Oslo. The third phase of her life's work began, but she did not cease to play a leading role in the international communist women's movement. Probably she owes her survival, at a time when her political friends "were disappearing" one by one, to this early transfer to the diplomatic service—long before the other inner-Party oppositional struggles—and to a certain shyness on Stalin's part to condemn prominent women. Her diplomatic activity was extremely successful. The first trade treaty between Norway and the Soviet Union concerned the delivery of Norwegian herring and in general was considered as extraordinarily favorable to the Soviet partner. When on February 15, 1924, the Norwegian government recognized the Soviet Union, Alexandra Kollontai was appointed as the first ambassadress of her country to Oslo. When Soviet-Norwegian relations were normalized further, in 1927, she was sent as ambassadress to Mexico. Despite the successes of her activity in America she had to depart in June of the same year because she could not take the climate in a city lying 6500 feet above sea-level, and returned to her post in Oslo. During her period of service in Norway the Soviet embassay developed into a cultural and social center. Writers, actors, musicians, intellectuals, native and foreign politicians met with the highly cultivated, worldly, and open-minded woman diplomat. Trygve Lie, later general secretary of the United Nations, knew and esteemed her. She enjoyed a similar success in Sweden, where she was active from 1930 up to her retirement in 1945 as minister and ambassadress (in 1943 the legation in Stockholm was raised to the rank of embassy). As a member of the Soviet mission to the League of Nations she elaborated questions dealing with the legal status of women. During the Soviet-Finnish war she managed to prevent the tension which had developed in Swedish-Russian relations from leading to an open break. "It was owing to her efforts that the peace treaty was signed between Finland and the Soviet Union on March 13, 1940," according to Itkina. Alexandra Kollontai was again active as a mediatrix at the conclusion of the Armistice between Finland and the Soviet Union in August of 1944. She made a major contribution to those initiatives that made it possible for Finland to withdraw from the war and preserve its independence (V. Kekkonen). The woman writer Hella Woolijoki, whose character "Herr Puntila" in the play *Puntila and His Servant, Matti,* written in collaboration with Brecht—and a world-wide staged success—also acted as a mediatrix between the Finnish foreign minister and Alexandra Kollontai.

Obviously, the fascination of this extremely attractive personage —as revolutionary fighter, as democrat, as feminist and sex-reformer, as woman diplomat and art enthusiast—was not exerted only on her old friends and acquaintances. A film on her life is being prepared in the Soviet Union. It is to be hoped that the contradictory, lively personality of Alexandra Kollontai will not be trivialized and pettified. Her brief autobiography, written in 1926, is a contribution to the presentation of a demythologized image of her being and activity.

Bibliography

Important Publications of Alexandra Kollontai

"Basic Features of Education According to the Conceptions of Dobroliubov," in the periodical *Obrazovanie* (*Education*), 1898

The Life of Finnish Workers (*Zhizn' Finliandskikh Rabochikh*), 1903

Finland and Socialism (*Finliandia i Sotsialism*), a collection of articles, 1906

The Social Foundations of the Women's Question (*Sotsial'nye Osnovy Zhenskogo Voprosa*), 1909

Worker Europe (*Po rabochei Evrope*), 1912

Society and Maternity (*Obshchestvo i Maternstvo*), 1913

Who Needs War? (*Komu nuzhna voina*), 1916

The New Morality and the Working Class (*Die neue Moral and die Arbeiterklasse*), Berlin, 1920

The Workers' Opposition in Russia (*Die Arbeiter-Opposition in Russland*), with critical notes by R. Korpelanski, member of the Revolutionary Workers Opposition (KAP) of Russia, Berlin, O/J. (1921). Reprinted according to the text of the Russian original (*Rabochaia Oppozitsia,* Moscow, 1921) in *Arbeiterdemokratie oder Parteidiktatur,* edited by Frits Kool and E. Oberländer, Olten u. Freiburg i. Br. 1967, pp. 182–240

Report at the Third Congress of the Comintern (Moscow, June 22–July 12, 1921), *Protocoll des 3. Kongresses der K. I.,* Hamburg 1921, pp. 776–781

Wege der Liebe, Berlin (Malik Verlag), 1925

"Ziel und Wert meines Lebens," "The Aim and Worth of my Life," in *Fuhrende Frauen Europas,* 1st Series, published by Elga Kern, Munich, 1926

Works in English Translation

Communism and the Family, London, 191?
Free Love, translated by C. J. Hogarth, London, 1932
A Great Love, translated by Lily Lore, New York, 1929
Red Love, New York, 1927
The Workers Opposition in Russia, Chicago, 1921